HARRY C

HE
OF THE
NORTH

David Clasper

GATESHEAD BOOKS

(From the Portcullis Press)

First published in Great Britain in 1990 by Gateshead Books

Copyright © Gateshead MBC

ISBN: 0 901273 13 9

British Library Cataloguing-in-Publication Data
CIP Catalogue Record for this book is available from the British Library

Printed and bound in Great Britain by BPCC Wheatons Ltd

Published in association with Portcullis
Press, Gateshead Metropolitan
Borough Council, Libraries and
Arts Department

GATESHEAD BOOKS

An imprint of Wheaton Publishers Ltd

Wheaton Publishers Ltd
Hennock Road, Marsh Barton, Exeter, Devon EX2 8RP
Tel: 0392 411131; Telex 42794 (WHEATON G)

SALES

Direct sales enquiries to Gateshead Books at the address above

This book is the result of David Clasper's own research.

Cover Photograph: Harry Clasper

To my wife Jean, without whose tireless
help and patience this book would never have been written

CONTENTS

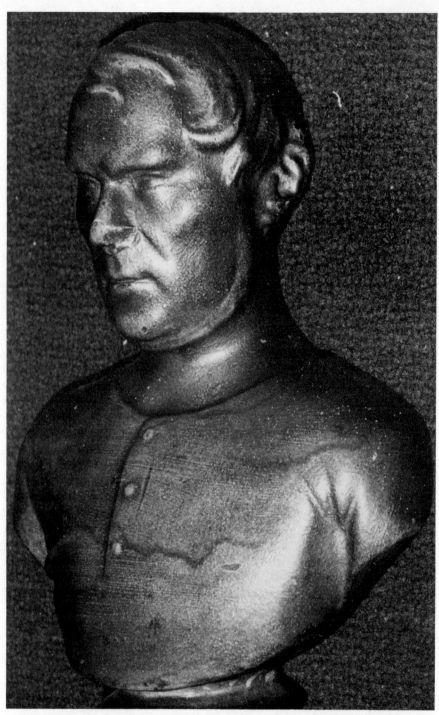

The bronzed plaster bust of Harry Clasper given to David Clasper by his Aunt Maude.

PREFACE

I can remember as a youngster visiting my Aunt Maude. Her main topic of conversation was, as she put it, her 'famous ancestors'. She would talk for hours of stories that had been passed down to her about their exploits against the best rowers of the day. It seemed if you were prepared to sit and listen, she could go on all day. As I grew older I took more interest, but her memory was by then starting to fail her, and she would often repeat one or two of the stories, and forget about the others.

A few years ago my aunt died and bequeathed to me a bronzed plaster bust of Harry Clasper, which had been her pride and joy. Also at about that time, a statue of Harry came up for auction, and I was lucky enough to purchase it. This was when I really started delving into the family's history. With help from my wife, sister, and two cousins living in the South, I followed up every lead we could find, and we were soon hooked on the exciting lives of the famous Claspers.

Harry, the best known of the brothers, was their leader. He was my great-great-uncle, his younger brother Richard being my great-grandfather. Richard was the cox in the boat when they won the Championship of the World on the Thames in 1845, but was also a great rower in his own right. He held the record for covering the championship course on the Tyne from the High Level to the Scotswood Suspension Bridge in the shortest time. This record was set in his match against Mathew Taylor in 1852 — the time returned being 20 minutes and 10 seconds.

We have spent many hours sifting through old newspapers in local libraries, and going through the parish records and census forms trying to track down where they all lived. Even the local cemeteries, although not the best of places to spend a Sunday afternoon, came in for some close scrutiny. It was fascinating, and the more we researched the more we were hooked. My sister found that even a steam tug-boat had been named the *Harry Clasper*. The extraordinary feature of the boat was the organ that she carried, which was played by the wind, and amongst the lively tunes to which she treated the neighbourhood as she plied up and down the river, was 'Pop o' Dilly Hornpipe'. Her figurehead was a likeness of Harry.

1

View of the Tyne and Newcastle showing the High Level Bridge.

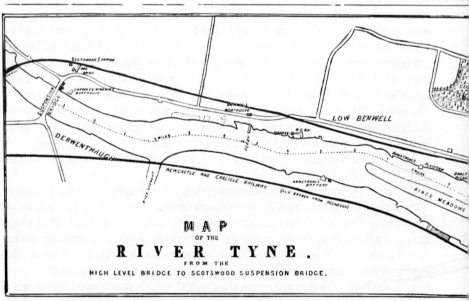

Map of the River Tyne showing the course from the High Level Bridge to Scotswood Suspension Bridge.

Scotswood Suspension Bridge on the Tyne.

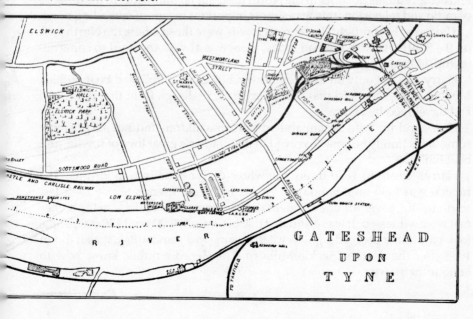

Although there is still a long way to go, and many more years of hard work to make our journal complete, I felt I had to put into short story form the lives of our local heroes.

The name of Harry Clasper may not be known by many people living in the North of England today, but between the 1840s and 1870s it was as famous as those of Steve Cram and Brendan Foster.

The North East of England in general, and Newcastle in particular, was fast becoming heavily populated — the growth of heavy industry bringing many people out of the country areas into the great city. This gave Harry a ready-made audience. Crowds of between 50 000 and 100 000 would line the banks of the river to watch a major race, and sculling was soon to become as popular then as professional football is today.

Harry's greatest success was in 1845. He went to London with his brothers to take on the Thames watermen, until then the undisputed Champions of the World. The Claspers won, and brought the championship north to the River Tyne for the first time. The scenes on their return to Tyneside have never been equalled. It seemed as if the whole city had turned out to welcome them back home. The Geordie public has always saluted the local lad who makes good. It seems 'wor Harry' may have been the first in a long line of local heroes.

Harry was very popular amongst the general public and no matter where he or his brothers were rowing there would be large crowds cheering them on. Because Harry became such a focal point, popular culture followed him and many song writers such as Geordie Ridley and Joe Wilson featured his exploits in their work. This helped to spread the news of Harry's endeavours and achievements not only in the North East, but far and wide. In the absence of radio and television, this was a most important means of spreading news.

The races that brought the largest crowds were those where the North took on the South. As with football today, there was always the need to come out on top, to beat the southerners.

Harry was not only an excellent rower, but an accomplished boat builder. Modern racing boats (skiffs) differ very little in design from that pioneered and developed by Harry.

Harry and his wife Susannah had thirteen children and not surprisingly some of his family became involved in their father's great love of rowing and boat building.

Harry's death in 1870 threw the whole of Tyneside into mourning. The funeral was held on a Sunday to enable his many friends to pay their last respects. But never for one moment did the organizers anticipate the scenes that were witnessed. It was estimated that between 100 000 and 130 000 people took part in the proceedings. Newcastle came to a standstill, just as it did in 1988 after the death of Jackie Milburn. The Geordie public know how to honour their own.

David Clasper

INTRODUCTION

By Denise Wilson

Origins and Development

To assess the popularity of the Tyne boat races one has only to read a contemporary observation of such an event:

> The ringing bells proclaim the approach of the hour for a great aquatic 'event'. The heart of the town is convulsed, the stations teem with unfamiliar forms and faces – the river steamers groan under their living freights – the cab wheels rattle over the granite roadways – the sound of the forge dies away and the blast of the furnace is unheard – the counting house and desks are deserted, and the academic benches are vacant. Eager crowds throng the streets and hasten to the banks of the only 'coaly Tyne'. Men of all cliques, classes and colours are there – Radical and Tory Quayside merchant and slouching loafer – master and servant – the great whitewashed and the 'great unwashed' are there, nay even women and children join in the hurrying to and fro…
>
> The High Level Bridge and Redheugh Bridge each bears seething masses of humanity; the Rabbit Banks on the south and the ballast mounds on the north are thronged with spectators, while other crowds amid the foliage of Redheugh Hall… It still remains to hear the ringing cheers of welcome and encouragement that greet the first dip of the oars that are engaged in doing battle for the honour of Tyneside.[1]

There are a number of speculations about the advent of the boat race on the River Tyne. It could be said that wherever there is a large river you may find people taking up boating, yet there existed a tradition of events that took place on the river for many centuries. After a long, hard day's work down the mines, on the river, or in the factories, an evening of watching river racing was a means of relaxation. Crowds of people would pack the narrow lanes and streets on the way down to the river. People from all walks of life would be interested in the racing and often a great deal of gambling would take place on the outcome of the evening's sport.

Many oarsmen in the famous boat races began their careers in the sport as the result of a wager amongst friends. In 1856 a few friends of Teasdale Wilson clubbed together a few shillings to back him in a local match for 10s. a side. Later in his career he was competing for prizes of £20 to £100 a side.[2]

As the sport became more popular, the races occurred with greater regularity and contestants came from all over the country and indeed the world, to row against the celebrated heroes of the North.

The Clubs — Amateur and Professional

The three major rowing clubs of the 1860s, when boat racing on the River Tyne was at its peak, were the Tyne Amateur Rowing Club (T.A.R.C.), the Northern Rowing Club, and the Albion Club. The Tyne Amateur Rowing Club was composed of what was considered the upper class of amateurs; the Northern Rowing Club had no restrictions, 'both landsmen and watermen alike being on a footing'. The Albion Club had the same open constitution but was composed mainly of 'landsmen' (workers on land as opposed to water). The success of the clubs was in the main put down to 'the startling victories of the Claspers, who had won the Tyne a name for her watermen'. The T.A.R.C. was formed in the mid 1840s and by the 1850s and 60s the club was well established, having 104 members by 1865, among them the Duke of Northumberland. The club was extremely well organized, having life, honorary, and yearly membership. Each season they held elections where the club officials would be appointed. These would include a president, two vice-presidents, a secretary, treasurer, captain, lieutenant and a committee of management of six people. All new members had to be nominated in writing by two existing members. Life membership was 5 guineas plus 1 guinea entrance fee. These stipulations were obviously out of reach of the ordinary worker.

The club had a constitution and an events calendar for the rowing season, which ran from the first Monday in April to the last Monday in October. The season would open with a string of formal and informal dinners, fêtes and processions. On one such occasion, '... an alfresco dinner was enjoyed by all, with refreshments at the Ferry Boat Inn with entertainment by Thomas Watson, a cornopean performer'. They also held an annual dinner, usually at the Royal Turks Head, Grey Street, costing 7s. 6d. per head. The club uniform was as follows: 'White jerseys with black facings, white flannel trousers with black binding. A white straw hat with a white ribbon embroidered with the initials T.A.R.C., also a blue pea jacket and vest with regulation club buttons, as undress, a white flannel cap trimmed and marked in black with the club insignia in the peak.'[3]

A list of members in the club's annual report of 1862 shows the occupations of the men as follows:

Bagnall, Joshua	Wheat Sheaf Inn, 6–8 Cloth Market
Blackett, R.	B. & Wilsons

Burnett, T.	T.B. & Sons
Curry, Mr	Garricks Head Inn, 40 Cloth Market
Fothergill, R.T.	Lampblack Manufacturer
Hutchinson, James	Oil Merchant
Ions, W.J.	Professor of Music
Jobling, M.L.	Solicitor and District Registrar, Court of Probate
McAllum, Ch.	Merchant
Pickett, T.J.	Wine, Spirit and Ale Porter Merchant
Reveley, Wm Jnr	Wine, Spirit and Ale Merchant
Wilson, D.H.	Bookseller
Ord, Mr	House Surgeon
Bolton, A.	Solicitor
Doeg, Mr	Ship Broker and Coal Fitter
Dryden, Mr	Tallow Chandler and Soap Merchant
Garland, J.	Watchmaker and Jeweller
Henderson, Mr	Ship Owner
Hills, Ed	Colonial Agent
Johnson, Wm	Gentleman
Liddell, H.	M.P., London
Mau, Mr	Geipal & Co.
Milvain, J.	Gentleman, North Elswick Hall
Newcombe, F.	Agent
Pearson, Wm	Draper and Tailor
Parker, T.	T. & Co. Chemical Brokers
Watson, J.	Inn Keeper [4]

It is easy to see from this list that the members of the club were mainly professionals and merchants, and dealers in the drink trade.

There were other clubs similar to this all over the British Isles. In Scotland there were the Phoenix and Clydesdale clubs. In England there were hundreds in the North alone; every area appears to have had its own amateur rowing club — Stockton, Tynemouth, Durham, Tees, Hartlepool and York to name a few. Each club held its own regatta and invited other clubs to take part. However there does appear to have been an element of elitism involved. Note the following letter addressed to the T.A.R.C. from the Cork Harbour Rowing Club, dated 19 July 1862.

Dear Sir,
    May I beg to call your attention to the following race for four-oared boats of any class, outriggers excepted, but if the boat be made in three or more streaks, a short outrigger on the bow and stroke oar will be permitted. To be rowed and steered by Gentlemen Amateurs, who must be members of a recognised Yacht or rowing club or Officers in the Army or Navy. *Working Mechanics excluded.*[5]

It would appear that as the sport developed it became less segregated, members of the different clubs officiating at other clubs' races. All of the clubs as a group appear to support individual oarsmen from the Tyne who took part in national and international matches. Indeed men from all classes could participate in the same sport and learn from each other, this being especially apparent in the case of Harry Clasper, whose expertise on all rowing matters shot him up the social ladder, to be respected by 'the great whitewashed and the great unwashed' alike.

Drink, Gambling and the Sporting Press

It has become fairly obvious that many of the backers of the oarsmen were involved with the drink trade. Renforth was backed by Blakey, who owned the Adelaide Hotel; Joshua Bagnall, who was proprietor of the Oxford Music Hall, was also a principal supporter and president of the N.R.C. — he owned numerous public houses throughout Newcastle and Gateshead. The system of backing was usually highly complex; here is an example of the arrangements for a match that took place in 1860 between Harry Clasper and George Drewitt of London:

> H. Clasper begs to inform G. Drewitt that he will give or take £10 for expenses and toss for choice of place and row him for £50 or £100. The race to come off within 3 months from the first deposit. Articles to be sent to Clasper and deposit to *Bells Life* will at once be attended to 15th January 1860.

In reply:

> White Swan, Newcastle, 23rd January 1860.
> Articles of agreement between H. Clasper of Newcastle-upon-Tyne and Geo. Drewitt of Chelsea to row a sculler match for £100 a side from High Level Bridge to Scotswood Suspension Bridge, on Tuesday 8th May 1860, one hour before high water, £10 to be allowed by Drewitt for expenses and to be paid on his arrival in Newcastle by applying to Mr Morrow, White Swan, £10 a side to be made good at Mr Morrow's on 4th February. The next deposit of £10 a side at Mr Wilcox on March 17th, £10 a side to be made good at Mr Clasper's, Boat Inn, Gateshead. 3rd March £10 a side to Mr Wilcox, White Hart, Barnes. £10 a side to Mr J. Bagnall, Nuns Gate on 31st March. Mr Wilcox on April 14th, £10. The next £10 at Mr Morrow's on the 28th April and the final deposit of £30 a side to be sent to the editor of the *Era Newspaper*, London. Either party failing in this agreement forfeits the whole money down. The referee to be chosen on the morning of the race.
> Mr H. Park for Harry Clasper.
> Mr Jewett for Geo. Drewitt.

Drewitt won in 22 minutes and 18 seconds. Harry Clasper received £7.8s. which was collected for him on board the officials' and spectators' boat the *Louise Crawshay*.

Newspapers were sometimes condemned for encouraging gambling, but they did play a large part in promoting races, and the sporting columns, as in the match between Clasper and Drewitt, often included the deposits for the matches.

Denise Wilson has carried out extensive research on the social history of rowing on Tyneside.

REFERENCES

1   Lawson, *William D. Lawson's Tyneside Celebrities:* sketches of the lives and labours of famous men in the North. Newcastle, William D. Lawson, 1873, p. 315.

2   *Newcastle Daily Chronicle*, 13 February 1863.

3   Rules of the Tyne Amateur Rowing Club, 16 February 1859, in *Tyne Amateur Rowing Club 1859–1865*, R. W. Martin.

4   Tyne Amateur Rowing Club Report, 1862, in *Tyne Amateur Rowing Club 1859–1865*, R. W. Martin.

5   A scrapbook of newspaper cuttings, etc. relating to sport, sporting events, particularly rowing events, 1859–1879. 3 Volumes. Newcastle City Libraries and Arts.

Newcastle and the Tyne, where Harry Clasper spent hours wandering around among the docks and the boats.

1
THE EARLY YEARS

In the early 1800s a son was born to Robert Clasper and Jane Hawks. Little did the North East of England then know that they would soon have a new folk hero.

It is not known exactly when the Clasper family came to the parish of Whickham, but we do know that on 2 August 1807, Robert Clasper married Jane Hawks in St Mary's Church, Whickham. Jane was related to the wealthy Hawks family from Gateshead, who founded the celebrated iron works, and were involved in just about every iron construction of those days.

It was here in Jarrow that young Harry went to school, and when he wasn't at school he could always be found playing by the riverside. From a very early age life on the river fascinated him.

When Harry reached the age of fifteen, he, like many other young boys, was to find work down the mines. The notorious pit of Jarrow, well known for its dangers and explosions, was to be his place of employment. Fortunately for Harry, he left the pit just before several explosions occurred — one of which claimed more than fifty lives.

He next went to learn the trade of ship's carpenter. Because of Harry's character and practical ability he was able to pick out useful pieces of knowledge from his fellow work mates, and use these to his own advantage, especially in the construction of sailing and rowing craft.

When Harry was twenty-one, he went to work as a coke burner at Derwenthaugh. After a short stay there he moved on to work at the great iron works of Messrs Hawks, Crawshay & Sons of Gateshead. It was at about this time that a young lady called Susannah Hawks (who was in fact Harry's cousin), caught his eye, and they soon married. Susannah came from a wealthy family and was well educated, but Harry could neither read nor write.

Harry and Susannah were both overjoyed when their first son was born, and in order to please both sets of grandparents, they named him John Hawks Clasper.

Harry Clasper as a young man.

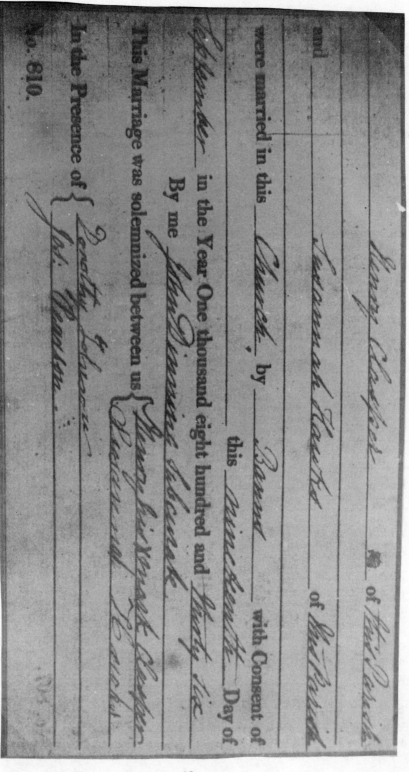

Henry Clasper .... of Portobello

and ....

Susannah Raper .... of Portobello

were married in this _Church_, by _Banns_ ....

.... this _Nineteenth_ Day of

September in the Year One thousand eight hundred and _thirty six_

with Consent of ....

By me _John Dunn, Curate_

This Marriage was solemnized between us {
Henry Susannah Clasper
Susannah Raper
}

In the Presence of {
Dorothy Lowcer
Jos. Beaden
}

No. 810.

Harry and Susannah Clasper's marriage certificate, which shows that at the age of twenty-five, Harry could not write.

13

At the age of twenty-five, Harry found that the strong pull of the river and the boats he loved was taking over his life. He was often seen pulling in a boat on his native River Tyne, and it was not long before he and his brothers were putting together a crew. Their first attempt at boat racing was around 1837. Harry rowed in a boat called the *Swalwell*, with his crew of William Clasper, John Thompson, Robert Dinning, Robert Clasper (coxswain), and himself stroke. They were victorious, beating a celebrated Swalwell crew, who rowed in a boat named the *Country Lass*. The prize was only small in rowing circles, being somewhere in the region of £10, but the victory at once brought the Claspers into note as a powerful crew.

Although every spare minute he had was taken up with his love of boats, Harry still had a family to feed and he became an employee of the Garesfield Coke Company, Derwenthaugh, as a wherryman. At last he had a job that involved boats and the river. Surprisingly he did not stay in this line of employment very long, and moved with his family to take up the tenancy of the Skiff Inn in Derwenthaugh, where he became a publican. A strange choice of employment perhaps, but we can only assume that this was to give him more time for the sport he loved.

The inn stood at the end of a row of houses, running in line with the railway. In front of the house, alongside a large pond, stood his boat building establishment. It was there in 1840 that he built a boat named *The Hawk*. In 1841 he built *The Young Hawk*, in which he won the Durham Regatta in 1842.

An annual regatta was set up on the River Tyne by the Corporation of Newcastle. All the local crews competed. Not surprisingly, Harry and his crew took the honours — it was rare to see them beaten. Year after year they came out on top, and became the undisputed Champions of the Tyne. In fact they became so successful that very few local crews would row against them. It seemed that the Tyne watermen were of the opinion that Harry's victories were attributable to the excellence of his boat the *St Agnes* — built by John Dobson of Hillgate, Gateshead, around 1840.

Harry and his friends tried to find new opposition outside of the area, and put out a challenge to the Thames watermen, who were the undisputed national champions. When they realized that it was a serious challenge, they accepted, and travelled north.

The race took place on 16 July 1842. The stakes were set at £150 a side, and the distance to be rowed was from Newcastle Bridge to Lemington. The Derwenthaugh Crew (as Harry and his men were known) rowed in their boat *St Agnes 1*. The Thames men (or London crew) consisted of Newell, Coombes and J. and R. Doubledee. It turned out the race was easily won by the London men, in a time of 29½ minutes. Naturally they were jubilant, and hoped that all those who had witnessed the race would not deny them their rightful place as national champions.

Harry accepted the defeat, but knew in his own mind that its cause lay in the construction of the *St Agnes* and not in the rowing of his crew. With his wife's help he had been working in the evenings on a new boat, which he would much rather have used to row against the London watermen.

However, it appeared to be too new a concept for the old keelmen of the river, who advised him against using it in the race. In Harry's opinion the *St Agnes* was about double the weight of the London boat, and every pound of extra weight was an additional burden upon the muscles of his crew. They had been handicapped out of the race. Deep down in his heart he knew that the four-oared boat he had almost finished was to change the whole structure of racing craft. The boats that carried oarsmen in prize rowing races in many cases were working boats. These would play their part in the industrial business of the river by carrying goods or passengers from place to place. Harry knew that they were heavy work-a-day boats, difficult to steer and, in general, very clumsy. He was sure in his own mind he was right and his new design of boat would revolutionize the sport of rowing.

Harry continued taking part in the local races, while his friends tried for other competition. In August 1843 Harry took part in the Tyne Regatta. With his brothers he won the four-oared race and on his own he won the Silver Cup. However, in June of the following year there came the race meeting for which Harry and his crew had been training long and hard. It was the Royal Thames Regatta. He was going to prove to the London watermen that he and his brothers were a crew to be reckoned with. He took with him the boat that he had started to build in 1842, and which was recently completed. Her name, quite appropriately, was *The Five Brothers*, and there was no doubt it created a great deal of speculation and excitement amongst the London watermen and their supporters. Her construction was quite revolutionary. According to the London watermen's ideas of racing vessels, it would be impossible to row her steadily because she was shaped like half a gun barrel. As it turned out this was to be the first keel-less boat ever built, and the first time that outriggers were used on a boat on the Thames. *The Five Brothers* was to be the forerunner of our present day racing craft. Outriggers were normally made of iron and fitted to the side of the skiff; across these would lie an oar. As a result the rower had more control of his craft. The first outriggers used in racing were fixed on a boat called the *Diamond* of Ouseburn, Tyneside. She rowed against the *Fly* of Scotswood-on-Tyne in the year 1828. But these outriggers were only rude pieces of wood, invented by Anthony Brown of Ouseburn and fixed to the sides of the boat by a boat builder named Ridley. In the same year Frank Emmet claimed the invention as his own, but it was Harry who perfected it. In the end the idea became associated with Clasper alone.

Until Harry had been defeated in that first four-oared race between the Claspers and the London watermen in 1842, he had used a perfectly straight oar. The London watermen rowed with a scoup oar, and Harry believed that this had also give them an advantage. As a result, Harry set to work and adapted his own oars. In *The Five Brothers* he knew he had not only a beautiful craft, but with the help of a good crew, one that was capable of taking on and beating anyone.

Harry and his crew carried off the £50 prize at the Thames National Regatta on 22 June 1844. It was generally believed that had his young coxswain, Harry's brother Richard, not made a slight error with the navigating, they

An advertisement taken from The Almanack of 1863 showing that Harry Clasper became recognized as the inventor of the outrigger.

16

would also have brought the Championship of the World away from the Thames. There was now no doubting the skill and power of the crew. They carried on winning in many local regattas that year. But Harry still eagerly awaited a race that had been fixed up on the Tyne against the Thames champion rower Robert Coombes. This was the race all Tyneside had been waiting for and it was to be rowed for £180 from Newcastle Bridge to Lemington. Arrangements were made, including depositing the prize money in small amounts with Mr Clayton of London, and the race was set to take place on 18 December 1844. It was agreed that Coombes' backers would put up £100 to Harry's £80.

As the day of the race dawned, there was a great deal of excitement with the quay and its side streets buzzing with activity. There were people from all walks of life vying for the vest vantage points to see the race, and the noise amongst the crowds was deafening. After all, it was a race between the Champion of the Tyne and the Champion of the Thames. As the two rowers took their places on the river, betting was brisk on which rower would be victorious.

As the race got under way the crowd could see it was going to be a hard-fought battle. Both rowers were matching stroke for stroke. Then the worst possible thing happened. Harry had the misfortune to run foul of a keel boat at Skinner Burn, and from that moment the race was lost. Coombes rowed home to the loud cheers of his supporters. Harry rowed on gamely but was beaten at the end by about six boat lengths. It was said by one spectator that Coombes had rowed so tight on Harry that he had had to alter his line and had therefore collided with the keel boat. But Harry had no complaints. He accepted defeat.

Both boats had been built specially for the race. Coombes' boat weighed 43 lb, and Harry's weighed 49 lb. The day after the race, friends of Coombes proposed that he and Clasper should try their skill again in another skiff race the following week. They offered to stake £200 on behalf of Coombes to Harry's £100. The challenge was accepted and £20 was deposited with Mr Joseph Hair of the Quayside by Coombes and £10 by Harry. The balance of the money was to be deposited within three days. Harry's friends were ready with their money, but the other party failed to fulfill their part of the agreement, although they were the challenging party. As a result, Harry claimed and obtained the forfeited £20.

The racing year was drawing to an end. It had been a most successful one for the Claspers, but now they had to set their sights on the following year and the start of a new season. The big event for them was to be the Thames Regatta on Thursday, 26 June 1845.

Harry had built a new boat for the Thames Regatta which he named the *Lord Ravensworth*. It was a beautiful boat, and was thought by some to be the finest boat he had ever built. Unfortunately, one crew member, Harry's brother Edward, died on 1 April 1845 aged only twenty-five. Harry therefore had to replace him with his uncle, the 'old 'un', Ned Hawks. Edward Clasper was going to be greatly missed. Despite his wooden leg he had been a fine rower and a valuable member of the Clasper crew. Nevertheless, Harry, three of his brothers and Uncle Ned Hawks were determined not to be outdone this time.

It seemed that everyone at the Thames Regatta wanted to see the Claspers and their boat. The banks of the Thames were thronged with thousands of spectators. It was very noticeable that a lot of the London watermen had now copied the lines of Harry's boats (imitation being the sincerest form of flattery). The race was divided into heats, and two of the London crews made their way through to the final to do battle with the Claspers. The crews were made up as follows:

Robert Coombes' Crew
R. Coombes, T. Coombes, J. Phelps, T. Goodrun, D. Coombes (coxswain).

The *Lord Ravensworth* of Newcastle
H. Clasper, W. Clasper, R. Clasper, E. Hawks, Richard Clasper (coxswain).

London Crew
R. Newell, Pocock, Robins, Dodd, E. Maynard (coxswain).

They moved to the positions for the start of the race. It was remarked upon, by men of long standing in aquatic matters, that they had never seen such speed in four-oared boats. They not only started at the same instant, but after several rapid and hard pulls, they were oar for oar. As they neared the committee boat Coombes' crew began to show ahead, and when level with the committee boat were rowing with all their might. The Clasper and Pocock crews were on level terms with each other, with their heads level with Coombes' midships. At this point Mr Bishop (who was umpire for the race) was no longer accompanying the rowers, but was steering his cutter to come on board the committee boat. After boarding, he stated that the crews, on his having enquired if they were ready, went off, without being started by him. He had called to them frequently to tell them it was a 'No Race' but his calls had gone unheeded. As the race was very finely balanced he would now have to accept the result.

The Coombes crew were being pressed very closely by the Newcastle men. As the two boats came level with each other at about Crabb Tree, a great effort was made by the Coombes crew to take the lead. But as they approached Hammersmith Bridge the Claspers began drawing away and went about three boat lengths ahead. The Claspers supporters went wild with excitement, willing their boys home. Although the Coombes crew made a finishing spurt they were unable to take the lead again, and the Claspers came in first, winning by about one and a half boat lengths. Pocock's crew finished about three lengths behind the second placed boat. The crowds that lined the river banks joined in generously with the applause for the lads from the Tyne. Such scenes and noise had rarely been seen on the Thames.

As Harry and his crew lowered their oars into the water, and sank their heads into their hands amidst the noise, Lord Kilmorey — who was a great lover of aquatic sports — rowed alongside the Claspers and congratulated them upon their victory. He handed a silver tankard full of wine to Harry, who after tasting it, passed it to his brothers. When it was 'Willie's' turn to taste the wine, he emptied the tankard, exclaiming after having finished it, 'That's devilish good Porter', to the great amusement and astonishment of Lord Kilmorey and his friends.

The noise was still deafening as Harry and his brothers went to collect their £100 prize and with it the Championship of the World. Sir Lancelot Shadwell, Vice Chancellor of England, made the presentations. Lord Shadwell, in a witty aside, remarked that, 'Although the winners were Tyne men, the London watermen had not found them *tiny* competitors.' This went down well with the large crowd gathered around for the presentation.

On the following Monday, the Claspers (with the exception of Harry) arrived back at Newcastle from London to a fantastic welcome. It seemed that the whole of the city had turned out. They were greeted with a merry peal from All Saints' bells. The Gateshead bells also rang for the occasion and the guns at Hawks & Crawshay's works were fired. Flags were flown from several vessels on the river. The lads could not believe their welcome and were overcome by emotion. The Newcastle crew had not been outdone this time. They had become the true Champions of the World.

Harry had remained in London. He was not arranging another race, as a lot of people thought, but carrying out some shrewd business. He arrived back at Gateshead by train on the following Wednesday, bringing with him two commissions. One was to build a skiff for a private gentleman. The other was from Lord Kilmorey — to build a four-oared boat. His Lordship had already purchased the skiff the *Lord Ravensworth* for £81.

The excitement of this great Thames victory was not allowed to last. Not only had the Claspers to carry on with their everyday work, they also had to prepare for their next major races. The Great North of England Regatta was to take place on 21 July, and Harry and his crew practised as regularly as time would allow. They managed to carry off the first prize at the regatta, and Harry himself won the sculler's prize. It seemed that the Claspers were going from strength to strength. They were beginning to have problems fitting in all the challenges that were being made to them. After all, it was not every day that you could match your skills against the Champions of the World! Harry's friends had arranged for him to row against Thomas Carrol, the Champion of the Mersey, on the Mersey on 29 September for the sum of £200. Harry won easily — covering the distance in about 32 minutes with the winning distance being between 300 and 400 yards. It was rumoured that Carrol was suffering with boils at this time, and that he had offered Harry £20 a week, for two weeks, if he would postpone the match until he was fit again. Harry unfortunately had to turn down this request as he already had arranged a match with Mr John Coombes, a crack sculler from the Thames. However, as it happened, this match against Coombes did not come off.

Harry's support was growing. As a result some of his close friends and public figures of the area got together and presented him with a testimonial. He and his brothers were invited on 19 November 1845 to Mr Joseph Hare's

The start of a boat race from the High Level Bridge.

home at Spicers Lane, Newcastle, where the celebrated oarsman was presented with an elegant silver model of his skiff. He was also given a silver watch and a gold chain with a gold oar as an appendage, a pair of silver sugar tongs, and a dozen silver spoons! All of these were designed by Reid & Sons, a prominent jeweller of Newcastle. These gifts were given to Harry, 'as a token of respect for his ingenuity, perseverance, and upright conduct, on all occasions' by Mr James Dale Esq. A gold oar was also presented to each of his crew, namely, Edward Hawks, Robert, William, Richard and John Clasper.

Harry was not back in strict training because on 25 November 1845 he had a tough match against one of the top London watermen, William Pocock. The match was to be rowed for £100 a side. As usual, the money had to be deposited in small sums over a period of time. First £20 a side was deposited with Mr Wentrell of Lambeth. Next £30 was deposited with Mr Hairs of Quayside, Newcastle. A further £25 was left with Mr Wentrell, and the remaining £25 with Mr Hairs. The editor of *Bells Life* in London was to be the final stakeholder. *Bells Life* was a sporting newspaper published in London, and the editor was used frequently as stakeholder for many major aquatic races, with large amounts of money frequently deposited with him.

Harry had decided to row in the skiff with which he had contested the match against Carrol of Liverpool, and which he had built himself. The match was to be rowed on the Tyne from the Tyne Bridge to Lemington Point. With the race drawing near a great deal of excitement and interest was being generated. Harry was in excellent condition due to all his training, and looking forward very much to the race. Pocock arrived in Newcastle about a week prior to the race, and went straight into training. His skiff was built by Mr Wentrell of Lambeth and had been much admired by the public. Harry's skiff was covered completely with an oilskin like a canoe to prevent him shipping water if the river was rough. Pocock's was left open.

The day of the race arrived and thousands of spectators lined the banks of the river, all trying to get the best vantage point from which to view the race. A temporary grandstand, for better viewing, had been erected on the Kings Meadows. (The Kings Meadows was a narrow island about ¾ mile long in the middle of the river off Dunston. It has since been dredged away to allow all types of ships to come up to Armstrong's factories.) There was a strong breeze from the north-west, which caused a considerable swell, expected to favour strongly Harry, whose boat was built sharper and more suited for broken water. For some days prior to the race the betting was 5 to 4 on Pocock, but at the time of the start, odds were given as even money, which was eagerly accepted by the public. Shortly after 11 a.m. Harry made his appearance from the south side of the river, admidst the cheers of his friends. A few minutes later, Pocock embarked from the Old Mansion House, with cheers from a large party who surrounded him. On the river at this time were numerous small boats and craft of every description, too many to count.

At precisely 12 noon, the race was started. Harry went slightly ahead but was almost immediately headed by Pocock. A desperate struggle for the lead commenced at the Mansion House, and continued to the Skinner Burn, by

Kings Meadows on the Tyne. The island has since been dredged away to widen the river.

which time Harry had managed to get about three boat lengths ahead. After passing Elswick Staiths, Pocock made up some ground. Then the two parties fouled, but it was presumed that the circumstances were purely accidental, as they immediately recommenced the race. Pocock took the lead, but again fouled by rowing into the middle of some posts near the Herd's House. Pocock was quick to get free and continued the race at a good pace. He was closely followed by Harry, and at the foot of the Kings Meadows the two boats were side by side. Harry's enclosed boat took in little water; on the other hand, Pocock's shipped so great a quantity that he was forced to row on shore to empty it. His chance of success was consequently completely lost. Harry then had the choice of water and kept to the north side, which was comparatively sheltered, while Pocock, not being so well acquainted with the current, found himself in broken water several times. Harry took the remainder of the race very easily, and at the end was at least ¼ mile ahead. At one stage Harry was so far ahead, a steamboat captain on the river asked if he would like to go on board for a drink as he said, 'He would still have time to beat the leather britches from the Thames'!

The race was rowed in 35 minutes, and appeared to be highly satisfactory to rowers and spectators alike. When Pocock came up to the finish, he cordially shook hands with his opponent, amidst the repeated cheers of their respective friends. Pocock was immediately taken on board a steamer, and Harry rowed to Derwenthaugh, where he was warmly greeted by his admiring friends and neighbours.

The river police, assisted by a party from the town force, preserved excellent order throughout the whole race; and an officer was placed on board each steamer to regulate its speed, and thus prevent the inconvenience which had occurred on previous occasions, where the steamer had got too close to the rowers and its swell was felt to have affected the race. Notwithstanding the great swell, only one accident occurred, when a boat close to Derwenthaugh was upset. Another boat pulled to the spot, and with some difficulty saved the life of a wherryman named Ramshaw.

Harry had proved once again that on his day he was a match for any man, and that his boats were second to none. There was a lot of rejoicing that night and many a toast was raised to 'Had away Harry'. It was the last major race for Harry that year, and it had ended his season with a great success for Harry himself, for this boat and of course for his brothers. But the success of 1845 had to be forgotten, there was a new year and a new season to be approached. He had to build new boats, not only for himself and his crew, but for the many customers who now patronized him.

2
TRAINING AND FITNESS

As 1846 got under way Harry was putting the finishing touches to a beautiful eight-oared gig. By early April he had completed the craft. He launched her from his boathouse in Derwenthaugh in the presence of a large crowd. After the launch she was speedily manned by the Clasper and Burnett crews, and on the first stroke glided across the water beautifully amidst the loud cheers of the spectators. After rowing as far as Lemington, she returned to Derwenthaugh and was accompanied from there by a party of gentlemen in the *Laurel* steamer to Newcastle.

The boat was built of mahogany and was very highly polished. She was beautiful, 58½ feet long, and 2 feet 4 inches broad, and was made from the model of the celebrated *Lord Ravensworth*. Her appearance was greatly admired, and she was considered by some experienced watermen to be the largest and finest gig ever to be seen on the Tyne. Harry had built her to order for a party of students at Oxford University, and she was due to leave for her destination within the next few days.

In May a match was arranged for Harry to row against a top Thames sculler, Newell. This match was to take place on 22 June and, luckily for Harry, on his beloved River Tyne. It was very noticeable that Newell's craft, made by the London builders Wentrell & Company, had adopted Harry's successful method and fitted outriggers. He had also observed the cause of Pocock's defeat and had placed a piece of oilskin around the rower to prevent the craft being swamped. Harry had trained hard for the race and had been accompanied in exercising on the river by his young brother John. Many experienced watermen felt that John was so gifted in his style that he was the future champion of the Tyne.

As usual the occasion brought out the public in their thousands to cram the quays and the banks of the river. It seemed as though the district had been drained of its population and that the whole tide of life had flowed into the Tyne area. There was great concern that the Newcastle Bridge would collapse under the weight of spectators, not just because of the amount of people that

The poster advertising the `Great Rowing Match' between Harry Clasper and Newell, a top Thames sculler.

might have been hurt or killed, but also because its rival, the High Level Bridge, was not yet ready!

The directors of the Newcastle and Carlisle Railway Company were making the most of the occasion. They used scores of cattle trucks running on lines on both sides of the river, and promised to give the public a view of the contest throughout by keeping up with the boats in the race. But although they pocketed some thousands of sixpences, their promise of a good view of the race was not fulfilled! One short peep at the Redheugh Bridge and a second beyond the Kings Meadows was all that was seen by the passengers. A lot of complaints were made by the customers, who justly felt that they would have been in a much better position on foot than riding in a train which allowed the contending boats to shoot ahead and pass clean out of sight.

The race was a very close run affair, but Newell reached Lemington Point 40 to 50 yards ahead of Harry and won the race. Neither man seemed to be in much distress but it was evident that Harry looked rather jaded. His friends had said he was unwell when he started the race, having caught cold from exposure in the heavy rain on the previous Friday while out exercising in his skiff on the river. There was no getting away from the disappointment felt by Harry and his supporters despite it being a cracking race. Deep down, they knew if Harry had been well, he would have won. It only went to prove the sporting nature of the man, that he went ahead with the race despite feeling ill.

Harry was committed to racing. His races took up the best part of his life, and he could spend days travelling the length and breadth of the country by road, train or steamer to reach a race meeting. Luckily he had the help and support of his wife Susannah, who dealt with the day to day running of their inn.

It was on 16 November 1846 that Harry rowed against a local rival, Anthony Maddison, for £100 a side. Unfortunately however, this ended in a bitter dispute. Maddison fouled Clasper in the race. As a result, Clasper did not complete the course, and despite the referee insisting that Clasper should have the prize money, the stakeholder Mr William Teasdale refused to hand it over. Harry was advised by his friends to take this matter further, which he did. The court case went against Maddison and Mr Teasdale was forced to hand over the stake money and also pay the costs of the lawsuit.

There was also the strenuous training for himself, his crew, and other would-be rowers. He was a very hard taskmaster. The following is a copy of the very strict regime which he expected his many students to follow prior to any race:

When a young aspirant for aquatic honours presents himself, my first duty is to impress upon him the necessity of being quite in earnest about his work, that he must not underrate his opponent, and that he must lend me his willing aid in my endeavours to bring him to the best possible physical condition that his nature is capable of achieving. I then cheerfully ingratiate myself as his associate, study his mode of living, his likes and

A sketch of the boat race between Clasper and Newell.

27

dislikes, and accommodate his food, etc. to meet those circumstances. I generally have my friend out of bed between six and seven o'clock in the morning, and we proceed together on a gentle pleasant walk, conversing on any agreeable subject, while we perambulate a circuit of country of four or five miles, arriving at home about eight o'clock for breakfast. For this, the first meal of the day, we sit down with good appetites to a nice fresh mutton chop or a couple of fresh eggs and an agreeable cup of tea (we never drink coffee). After breakfast we rest for half an hour, and then, weather permitting, enjoy a smart walk or run, according to the constitution of the man undergoing training. If the morning exercise has not been heavy we enter the boats and have a good row on the river, always endeavouring to terminate the morning's work about eleven o'clock.

Our dinner, at mid-day, consists of beef or mutton broiled on the gridiron, and a light egg pudding, with currants in it if desired, or any other light farinaceous pudding. One glass of ale is allowed with dinner and a glass of port wine, or two glasses of ale without any wine, as taste may dictate. We take an hour's rest after dinner and then take to the boats again for a hard row, should the state of the tide be suitable. At all events, rowing exercise should be taken twice every day, once in the forenoon and once in the afternoon, taking care to time the rowing exercise about the time of day at which the match has to come off. I am particularly anxious to have as much rowing exercise as possible, because it not only brings the muscles that have to do the work into proper order, but I am generally enabled to improve my pupil's style of rowing. If my pupil be fleshy and not very hardy, I take care not to work him too much, as such a man loses strength fast if too rapidly reduced, and the mistake will only be discovered when it is too late to bring him into a hardy condition. A trainer must always exercise a wise discretion, and it is a folly to attempt to train a man by any set of rules. Some men who are not in good condition require good feeding and moderate work to bring them up to the mark. The work in short must be regulated according to the constitution and habits of the man, and the food, to a certain extent, must be adapted in a similar manner. Regularity of hours I insist upon, as indispensably necessary in proper training. To rise at seven in the morning and go to rest at ten at night are the times I generally fix, and I consider about three good meals per day a temperate and proper allowance – the third meal to consist of tea and toasted bread sparingly buttered, with one egg only – more than these has rather a tendency to choke the system. Some persons require a supper, and I would rather in such cases that the supper be as light as possible, say new milk and bread, or gruel with raisins or currants and a glass of port wine in it. Occasions may arise where a person must be brought down quickly (but this should be avoided if possible); in such cases, hard running or walking exercise while wearing an excess of clothing for a certain time; the pupil is then undressed, well rubbed down, and put into bed to undergo a further process of sweating, being well covered with bedding, and he may be kept there as long as circumstances may warrant. After this, he is again rubbed down until thoroughly dry and cool. He must now have a fresh supply of clothing, well aired and gently warmed. This rapid process of bringing a man into condition is not to be recommended, and should only be adopted in extreme cases.

It is fair to say that Harry took no chances that his crew could lose a race through their lack of fitness!

3
THE TROUBLED YEARS

In April 1847 a strange event took place. A young man by the name of John Bourne arrived in Newcastle. He was very respectably dressed and took up residence at Mr John Cox's Ord Arms Inn, Scotswood for the purpose of being trained by Harry to row a skiff match in Manchester. Mr Cox, in order to make his guest comfortable, gave up his own sleeping quarters in which was a chest of drawers containing a sum of money amounting to upwards of £200. Bourne's appearance was such that not the slightest suspicion was attached to him, until that afternoon, when the drawer containing the money, together with a cash box in which it was deposited, were found to have been broken open, and the entire contents removed.

Information of the robbery, with a full description of Bourne, was conveyed to Mr Stephens, the Superintendent of Police at Newcastle, who immediately put into operation the electric telegraph. When Bourne appeared on the platform of Normanton Station, he was immediately taken into custody, with the whole of the money still in his possession. He was tried at Northumberland Midsummer Sessions, and sentenced to ten years' transportation. As it turned out Harry had never heard of Mr Bourne, and Mr Cox wished he hadn't either.

In June 1847, following a very successful couple of days at the Durham Regatta where he won the pair-oared race with his brother John, Harry and his brothers were invited to the Grand Ball and large firework display.

Harry next accepted a challenge from Robert Coombes to row a pair-oared match for 100 sovereigns a side — Coombes and one of his brothers to row against Harry and one of his brothers. The race was to be rowed on the Thames or Tyne giving 25 sovereigns expenses to the travelling pair. There was a lot of hard work ahead for Harry. He not only had to build a new two-oared boat for his race against the Coombes brothers in August but he had also to pick his partner from amongst his brothers, and then organize their training. Everything was at last agreed and on 17 July the articles were drawn up. The race was to be between Robert and Thomas Coombes and Harry and Robert

Clasper. The toss for choice of venue was won by Coombes, who chose to row on the Thames, from Putney to Barker's Raile, Mortlake. The match was to be rowed on 11 August 1847. The race also had another peculiarity for the London crew. It was to be a coxed pair; this frequently occurred in provincial regattas, but very seldom on the Thames. A young 13-year-old boy, Henry Cownden, coxed for the Coombes brothers. The cox for the Claspers was their young brother Thomas, also aged 13.

The first deposit of £30 was made and it was agreed that the second £20 deposit be made at Mr Atkinson's, of Spicers Lane, Newcastle. The third deposit of £25 went to Mr Brown of Pipewellgate, Gateshead, and the final payment was deposited at the Red Lion, Westminster Road, within seven days of the race. The race was to commence half an hour before high water.

One of Harry's old friends happened to be in London that summer and on a sunny evening in July while strolling along the river's edge, he spied amongst the many other small craft the boat of Coombes and his brother, who were training for the approaching struggles with the Tyne champions. He informed Harry that they were in 'smart trim' and pulled very well together; this was a very important point in a double-handed match. At the same time as giving Harry this information about the opposition, his friend also mentioned a tip he had learned for the 'protection and comfort of the hands while using an oar'. It was to have a pair of wash-leather gloves soaked in oil, with another pair over them, to sleep in for two or three nights before rowing. It would put the hands into fine order and enable them to have a good pull on the oar without blistering; a tip Harry was very grateful for.

The day arrived for the match that was billed the Great Race — the Tyne versus the Thames. The event created a lot of excitement, and there were large crowds to give their support, many making the long journey from the North East. The race, which had been talked about all over the country, especially among the aquatic elite of London, Newcastle and Liverpool, proved one of the most exciting events seen for many years.

At 2.40 p.m. the umpires and referee took their places on the paddlebox of the steamer *Childe Harold*. The Coombeses first made their appearance afloat in a very beautiful outrigger built by a London man named Cownden. They exhibited the effects of fine training, and rowed in the following order: Robert Coombes, bow, weighing 9 stone; his brother Thomas, aft, weighing 8 stone 10 pounds; Henry Cownden, a boy of thirteen years of age, weighing 4 stone 5 pounds as coxswain. In the Claspers' boat Robert was forward, Harry aft and their young brother Thomas was coxswain. Pound for pound in their boats the Claspers were slightly heavier, giving their opponents the edge. The Claspers' boat, which Harry had just finished building, made them appear to sit on top of it rather than inside it, owing to its construction. As well as the difference in the two boats, there was also a considerable difference in their oars. The Coombes' oars were of ordinary shape and size, but those being used by the Claspers were of a totally new length and design. The biggest difference appeared to be in the length, which was 6 to 7 inches shorter than a standard oar.

*The skiff-shaped memorial to Harry Clasper's mother, father, and brothers
Edward and John in Whickham Cemetery.*

The race got under way at 2.45 p.m. The Coombeses jumped away with the lead, and stroke by stroke gradually drew away and after 180 yards were three lengths up. They went on to increase their lead and won by 46 seconds. The Claspers always tried to improve their position but without effect on this occasion. It seemed that there was still a lot of hard work to be carried out with this new style of oar. The oars were out of the water too long between strokes, the Coombeses getting four strokes in to the Claspers' three. Harry would have to think again about this oar.

This was just the beginning of what was to turn out to be a devastating time for Harry. Shortly after this bad result, Harry was to receive some distressing news. His younger brother John, aged twenty, and for whom Harry had a great deal of affection, died in tragic circumstances whilst at work. It seemed that he and another member of the family were navigating a wherry boat up to Derwenthaugh, when John slipped and fell into the river. It was thought that he hit his head on the boat as he went down and he never resurfaced. His body was not found until the following morning when it was discovered lying on the sands not far from the place where the accident happened. He was buried at Whickham Cemetery a few days later and placed in the same grave as his mother, father and brother Edward. The funeral procession was long, and followed by a great number of friends and relatives. Appropriately the grave was marked by a stone in the shape of an upturned prow of a skiff, which can still be seen today and bears the following inscription:

Beneath this unassuming stone
Lies one when living loved by all,
'Tis thus we dwindle one by one,
Obedient to our Maker's call.
His little skiff, his sole delight
Is now deserted, cast away,
His sculls he plied with skilful might
Are all now hastening to decay.
As brother none had stronger ties,
But now he's fled this busy world,
He's safely moored beyond the skies.
His match with time was ended soon,
The stakes were handed o'er with tears,
His death has caused a sudden gloom,
Which nought can dissipate but years.

It was also a very sad loss to the rowing world, as John, although still only very young, was hailed as the up-and-coming champion.

There was a dark cloud hanging over rowing and it appeared it would never go away. The loss of John seemed to take away all motivation, and it wasn't until the following June (1848) that the Claspers were back on the river. They took part in the Durham Regatta on 26 June and won the pairs, and in general had a good workout. This put them in good heart for the coming Thames Regatta.

Harry, with his brothers and friends, set off for London in a jovial mood. They were to contest the champion four-oared race with the same crew that had won the Durham Regatta in fine style, this being Harry, his brothers Robert and William and a close friend, J. Wilkinson. G. Oliver was to be coxswain.

As usual there were huge crowds on the day of the race and not surprisingly a large following from the North East. Harry had built the boat for his crew and called her the *St Agnes* after his first successful boat of the same name. It was another great day for the northerners, and with loud shouts of 'Had away Harry lad', the Tyne watermen once again carried away the £100 prize and the championship.

The following year, 1849, the Claspers took on, and beat, all comers. It was very rarely they lost a race. The Durham Regatta this year was to be another fine occasion for Harry and his brothers. Firstly in the coxed fours they carried off the Patrons' Plate and a purse of £30. Following this up with the coxed pairs, they took the Members' Plate with a purse of £10. They carried on their winning ways in other minor races. Harry also had the satisfaction of watching young Master George Hawks, son of the Mayor of Gateshead, win the Challenge Cup. Harry had been coaching George, and this was his first public appearance. The main feature of the year was another championship win on the Thames, taking the £100 prize, but this time being partnered by the Coombes brothers of London.

By 1850, Harry had left his licensed premises and boat house at Derwenthaugh, and taken up his new residence at the Queens Head in the Close. This meant he was more at the centre of things. He was within easy reach of his boating friends and could be involved even more in the setting up of the many races in which took part. He set up his boat house on the banks of the river near Redheugh and carried on with his building of fine craft. In 1851 Harry finished building a four-oared outrigger and launched it from his Uncle Edward Hawks' yard in the Close, Newcastle. It was a beautiful craft made of cedarwood and measured 42 feet in length and 21 inches in breadth. It was built for the use of Harry and his brothers in their competition for the champion prize at the Henley-on-Thames Regatta.

When the day of the regatta arrived Harry's boat was the central attraction. They were heading for a victory in the first race when a thowl (the part of the boat that the outrigger is fixed to) broke, putting them out of the race. They were not to be outdone, however. In a second race for fours they easily beat the Thames men — who were led by Robert Coombes. It turned out to be another splendid day for the Tyne lads and a fine regatta.

4
THE TOAST OF TYNESIDE

On their return to Newcastle, Harry's friends decided to honour their hero with an evening of entertainment. It was early July 1851 and with his brothers he was invited to his uncle Edward Hawks' house in the Queens Head Inn, Newcastle to commemorate their recent achievements in London.

Upwards of forty gentlemen sat down to a sumptuous supper. The chair was ably filled by Mr R. Riddle, and the vice-chair was held by Mr John Banks. After the table was cleared, and when the usual loyal toasts had been given and responded to, the chairman, in a highly complimentary speech, proposed the health of Harry and his crew. Harry replied on behalf of himself and his brothers in very appropriate terms and received great applause. A friend of Harry's, Mr Bagnall, next proposed the health of the veteran Edward Hawks which was warmly responded to by the guests. It turned out to be a good night for all.

Harry was now reaching the age of forty but was still a very fit man. Over the next three years he competed in many races covering the length and breadth of the country. His next great triumph was on 9 August 1854, when he easily beat Robert Newell in a sculls race on the Thames from Putney to Mortlake. There were loud cheers as Harry finished the race and collected the £100 prize. His winning streak continued, and soon after he partnered Pocock and won the pair-oared race at the Thames National Regatta. There was no doubting Harry's strength and his use of an oar. It seems that although older than his challengers he had lost none of his enthusiasm and skill for the sport.

Also in August that year he and his crew decided to row in the North of England Regatta. The day of the race arrived and the conditions seemed to be very unfavourable for rowing. In the morning there was torrential rain and this carried on until early afternoon. Owing to the bad weather the attendance was quite low, but those who turned up were kept entertained, watching the antics of a Dutchman and his crew who stole the show. The Dutch captain, Hisschenmoeller, was commander of the vessel *Le Nieuwe Rotterdamsche Gazfabrick*, lying in the Tyne. He and four members of his crew were loaned a skiff by the gentlemen of the Tyne Amateur Rowing Club, so that they could exhibit their aquatic skills. They appeared to be totally unused to the steering of such a light craft. Nevertheless, they rowed about for some time, to the great amusement of the spectators. They rowed a fair way up the river, then returned just ahead of the committee's boat. So confident were they by now that they decided to show off by raising their oars in the Dutch fashion. In doing so, their tiny craft turned over and gently placed the Dutch crew into the Tyne! There they struggled to get on to the boat. In doing so, they turned it round and soaked themselves again in the water. The captain, who had acted as coxswain, was the first to get out of the water by nimbly climbing astride the boat. The police boats and other small craft hurried to the spot and succeeded in rescuing the gallant sailors from a watery grave. They were brought on board the committee's boat, and supplied with cognac until they were once again warmed through! The captain and his crew were not disheartened by this mishap, laughed heartily at their adventure, and would have readily tried their luck once again in another boat. But the gentlemen from the rowing club very respectfully declined to have another boat damaged in a frolic, or risk the lives of the Dutch crew in a second adventure.

Getting back to the rowing, Harry paired with another local rower, Anthony Maddison, to take the £12 prize in the Watermen's Pair-Oared Race. In September friends and backers so enthused over Harry's victories and attitude to the sport that they arranged to honour him again. They met at Mr Blakey's Adelaide Hotel, Newcastle. A considerable number of friends turned up; every available seat and standing area was taken.

The purpose was to present *their* local hero with the whole of his stakes won in his latest contest on the Thames against his old rival Robert Newell. There was an excellent supper. The chairman, when presenting Harry with the stakes, took time to draw attention to the genius shown by him in the construction and improvement of wager-boats (these are working racing boats with no outriggers), and also to compliment him on his indomitable pluck and perseverance as an oarsman. He recalled how Harry had struggled on under difficulties which would have beaten down a man less resolute in mind. He had lived to see his system of boat building adopted wherever wager-boats were known, while he himself had turned the tables on the crack London oarsmen who originally had been so much his superiors. Before the proceedings closed a subscription list was opened for a testimonial to Harry and a large number of names were put down. The evening ended with loud cheering and applause for their local hero. Harry was one of the first of a long line of local sporting heroes idolized by the Geordies.

Harry carried on racing and building boats — the life he loved. He continued to win many major prizes, one being the Scullers' Championship on the Tyne in August 1855 and another against Mathew Taylor on the Tyne on 24 March 1856. He seemed to go from strength to strength, winning race after race. The Claspers became almost unbeatable through the seasons of 1856 and on into 1857.

In June 1858 Harry and his brothers took on the Taylors, and beat them by a considerable distance. This was an excellent warm-up race for their planned trip to Scotland. Harry was to take on Robert Campbell in a sculls race for £200 and the Championship of Scotland. It was a warm July morning when Harry left for Glasgow, planning to take in some exercise on the Clyde before his battle with Campbell. He was accompanied by one of his close friends, Robert Chambers, and also took with him one of the most beautiful examples of boat building art he had ever created. Was there ever a boat builder to compete with Harry? It seems each boat he built surpassed the last, in both its beauty and its structure. The boat in which he hoped to contest this match bore the unmistakable marks of his own personal craftsmanship. The dimensions were: length 33 feet, breadth a mere 10 inches, height of steer post 2 inches, weight only 33 pounds.

Harry was now in his forty-eighth year, but looked as vigorous as ever. His opponent, Campbell, was about fifteen years younger, and together with his muscular, athletic stature, this made him appear a formidable opponent. A great number of Harry's friends had made the journey to Scotland to watch this race, and the betting on the outcome was very heavy.

On the great day, 22 July, the weather was quite favourable although there had been a couple of sharp showers two hours before the start of the race. There was a very large crowd and a feeling of anxiety prevailed among the locals in case the best sculler that Scotland had ever produced should succumb to the prowess of a stranger. Harry did, however, have a slight edge in the betting. It was thought that even with Harry's great fame and former triumphs, Campbell's youth and strength would enable him to beat his opponent and win the day.

Because of the necessity of catching the tide at the ebb, the start was fixed for 10 a.m. The weather was fine and the river very busy. The *Petrel* and *Emperor* and three other steamers had brought down a considerable number of spectators from Glasgow and a crowd of small boats of all descriptions, their oars glistening in the sunlight, were seen skimming over the surface of the Clyde. As the hour for the start drew near, speculation was at its height. The friends of Campbell, probably on hearing a rumour that the veteran Harry could not 'stay' the distance, were venturing their money at evens on their favourite. As the two men came along slowly to the post, their condition and form were closely scrutinized. The condition in which Harry appeared at the starting point reflected great credit on his trainer, and Campbell too looked well and confident.

At about 10.15 a.m. a good start was made, both men darting off with great speed. Yet within a few strokes the nose of Harry's boat began to show in front, and the veteran soon drew his boat clear. He continued to increase his lead until 400 yards of the distance had been pulled, when one of the steamers followed so closely in the wake of Harry, that the surge from the paddles extended to him, and for a time considerably slowed him down. This allowed Campbell to come up, and for a second or two, the two skiffs were close together. When the water became smoother, Harry again shot ahead and

Robert Chambers — a top oarsman and Harry Clasper's closest friend, schooled by Harry to become a champion sculler.

regained his former position, eventually winning by about 250 yards. He pulled on the north side and Campbell on the south side of the course. The winning post was a boat bearing the Union Jack placed a distance of about 4 miles from the starting point. Around the finish was a swarm of about two hundred small boats filled with people who sent up a most enthusiastic burst of cheering. This was swelled by those on board the steamboats, as Harry came triumphantly past the winning post.

Although the race was of national importance there had been little doubt as to the result. Prevailing opinion gave Harry a great superiority over his opponent in the scientific knowledge of the art. The distance of 4 miles was pulled by Harry in 26 minutes. The ripple on the water didn't help Campbell, who took a short stroke, and, there being a swell, sunk his skiff deeper in the water, rendering greater exertion necessary. Harry, on the other hand, took a sweeping broad stroke which in such water caused the skiff to glide lightly over the waves.

While on board the steamer returning to Glasgow it was agreed that a second match be arranged between the two oarsmen, so that Campbell might have a chance of winning back his title. This was set up for the same purse but to be rowed on Loch Lomond, in early October. The race took place on the 6 October after being once postponed owing to the choppy conditions on the loch. Although Campbell rowed a lot better the result was the same — Harry won by 60 to 80 yards.

Harry had earned great respect throughout the rowing world. This was reinforced yet again in his last major race of the year. He was to row against a top London oarsman, Thomas White, on the Thames. While he was practising for this race, Harry was accidentally tipped out of his boat into the river. He had 4 miles to return to his lodgings, and in consequence caught a bad cold. Being the good sportsman that he was, this did not stop him from racing against White. But Harry could not give of his best, and was beaten.

Harry seemed now to be spending more and more time training his great friend and colleague Robert Chambers. He could see in Robert quite a lot of himself when he was the same age. With Chambers, Winship, his son John Hawks Clasper, and brother Richard as cox in their boat the *Lord Kilmorey*, his crew became practically invincible in the year 1859, winning at regatta after regatta all over the country. This included the big prize at the Royal Thames National Regatta, where they beat some of the finest rowers in the world.

As the season drew to a close, in October Harry and his crew were invited as guests to the formal closing day of the season dinner at the Assembly Rooms in Newcastle. It was on behalf of the Tyne Amateur Rowing Club and to show appreciation of the efforts on the part of the Tyneside watermen who had maintained the superiority of their river. As usually happened at these gatherings there were many toasts and speeches made throughout the evening. They started by toasting the first speech made by the chairman and carried on until they were toasting each other! When it came to the turn of Mr Septimus Bell, the retiring secretary and treasurer, he staggered to his feet

ROYAL NATIONAL

THAMES REGATTA.

PATRONS
HER MAJESTY THE QUEEN.
HIS MAJESTY THE EMPEROR OF THE FRENCH.
HIS MAJESTY THE KING OF THE BELGIANS.
HIS ROYAL HIGHNESS THE DUKE OF CAMBRIDGE.

Vice-Patrons.

DUKE OF ARGYLL.	MARQUIS or LONDONDERRY	EARL OF CHICHESTER.	LORD WHARNCLIFFE.
DUKE OF BUCCLEUCH.	MARQUIS of WESTMINSTER	EARL COTTENHAM	LORD FEVERSHAM.
DUKE OF BEDFORD.	EARL OF EGMONT.	VISCOUNT COMBERMERE.	EARL OF BELMORE.
DUKE OF NORFOLK.	EARL OF YARBOROUGH.	LORD DUFFERIN.	LORD STANLEY, M.P.
DUKE OF DEVONSHIRE.	EARL OF DURHAM.	LORD LONDESBOROUGH.	LORD ALFRED PAGET, M.P.
MARQUIS of BREADALBANE	EARL OF DENBIGH.	LORD COLCHESTER.	HON. W. F. COWPER. M.P.
MARQUIS OF DONEGAL.	EARL OF CARDIGAN.		

THOMAS CHAMBERLAYNE, Esq., Vice-Commodore, Royal Victoria Yacht Club.
President—THE RIGHT HONORABLE THE LORD MAYOR.

RACES, MONDAY, AUGUST 15th, 1859.

Sculler's Race.
(Open to the World.)

1st Boat £10; 2nd £5; 3rd £3; 4th £2.

The 1st and 2nd Boat in the 1st and 2nd Heat and the 1st Boat only in the 3rd Heat will row in the Grand Heat.

First Heat at 2.
1. R. Chambers, *Newcastle* ....Red & White
2. J. Chandler, *Hammersmith* ....White
3. J. Wise, *&c* ....Blue
4. W. Mancey, *Isleworth* ....Yellow

Second Heat at 2.30.
1. R. Piner, *Hammersmith* ....Green
2. G. Drewett. *Chelsea* ....Red
3. H. Kelley, *Fulham* .....Blue and White
4. T. Pocock, *Lambeth* ......Green & White

Third Heat at 3.
1. John Mackinney, *Richmond* ......Black
2. Thomas Mackinney, do. *Green & Red*
3. B. Oxlade, *Paul's Wharf, Yellow and Black*

Watermen's Apprentices.
For Coat, Badge, Freedom and Money Prizes amounting to £31.

1st Boat, Coat, Badge, Freedom and £2;
2nd £5; 3rd Boat £3; 4th £2.

(The Gift of the Thames Subscription Club.)

The 1st and 2nd Boat in each Heat will row in the Grand Heat.

This match is open to Apprentices from any part of the River without reference to the time they may have served.

First Heat at 3.20.
1. H. Styles, *Isleworth* ....White
2. J. H. Clasper, *Wandsworth* ......Black
3. F. Kelley, *Felham* ....Green
4. G. Francis, *Teddington* ....Blue
5. S. Beckett, *Fulham* ....Yellow

Second Heat 3.40.
1. J. Maloney, *Richmond* ....Red
2. H. Phelps, *Fulham* ...Green and White
3. E. Agars, *Chelsea* ...Yellow and Black
4. G. Shepherd, do. ....Red and White
5. W. Hemmings, *Richmond, Blue & White*

Champion Four Oar Race.
(Open to the World.)

For £105.

1st Boat £75; 2nd £15; 3rd £10; 4th £5.

(The 1st and 2nd Boat in each Heat will row in the Grand Heat on the following day.

First Heat at 4.
1. The Hammersmith Crew ....White
   J. Holder
   Y. Hoare
   R. Piner
   G. Green .... W. Hoare, Cox.
2. Lord Kilmorey Crew (*Newcastle*) *Blue*
   J. H. Clasper
   R. Chambers
   E. Winship
   H. Clasper .... R. Clasper, Cox.
3. The Shakespeare Crew (*Manchester*)
   H. Ault ....Red
   H. Lang
   E. Barratt
   F. G. Barratt ...... T. Barley, Cox.

Second Heat at 4.20.
1. The Adelaide Crew (*Fulham & Richmond*)
   F. Kelley ....Green
   T. Mackinney
   J. Mackinney
   H. Kelley .... J. Driver, Cox.
2. The Hampton Crew.................Yellow
   H. Snell
   G. Collis
   W. Moran
   J. Snell .... H. Everest, Cox.
3. The Western Crew (*Hammersmith*)
   G. Bullen ....Black
   T. Rust
   C. Gibson
   T. Wolsoncroft .... W. Norton, Cox.

(All the above Races are to be rowed up.)

The following Races will be rowed down.

Watermen's Apprentices.
Grand Heat at 5.40.

The Four Winners of the Trial Heats will contend in this Heat.

Sculler's Race.
Grand Heat at 6.15.

The Five winners of the Trial Heats will contend in this Heat.

---

1 The Distance for the Four Oar Races will be from Putney to Chiswick Eyot, and for the Sculler's Races from Putney to Hammersmith Bridge, or vice versa, according to the Tide.
2 The Numbers denote the Stations, beginning from the Surrey shore.
3 The Umpire's Boats will carry a White Flag, AND NO OTHER BOATS can accompany the Races under any pretence whatever.
4 The Races will be rowed up until 4.20, and the First Race down will be the Grand Heat of the Apprentices' Race at 5.40.
5 The Winners of each Heat will be announced by a flag similar to that carried by the winners, being placed in the Umpire's Boat, on its return to the Committee Barge after the Race, when the Colours will be hoisted on the Committee Barge, at Messrs. Searle's Boat Yard, and on Putney Bridge.
6 The Races will be started punctually at the time named on the Card; and every competitor or competitors not prepared to start at that time, will be distanced.
7 The Laws of Boat Racing, as settled by the Committee, will be strictly enforced.
8 The Committee will be in attendance on their Barge, throughout the day, from whom every information can be obtained.
9 Colours will be provided by the Committee; and will be given to the competitors at one o'clock.
10 The Umpires will start all the Races, and any Boat Starting before the Signal is given, will be declared to be distanced.
11 Two guns will be fired to clear the course three minutes before the time named for each Race to start, which will be the signal for the Boats to take their stations; and one Gun immediately after the start, which will be a notice for the Boats in the next succeeding Race to drop to stations. A Gun will be fired on the down Races approaching Putney to clear the course.
12 In all the Four Oar Races the Boats must be steered through the Middle Arch of Hammersmith Bridge.
13 The Umpires will draw the Stations for Boats in the Final Heats.
14 The Prizes will be presented on board the "Maria Wood" state Barge, at Half-past 6 o'clock.
The Band of the Royal Horse Guards (Blue) will attend, by the kind permission of Colonel Hon. C. B. Forrester, M.P.

By order of the Committee,   WALTER M. WALMISLEY, Sec.
Office—5, Victoria Street, Westminster Abbey.

Printed under the Authority of the Committee by H. P. BEDELL & Co, 1, Circus Place, London Wall.

The Royal Thames National Regatta in 1859.

and in a happy speech proposed the health of Chambers, the sculling champion and also the veteran Harry Clasper, and the remainder of the champion four. This was received with rousing applause. First Chambers stood up and thanked them for honouring him, and said how proud he felt at being invited to their banquet. He finished his speech promising he would fight with all his strength to keep his title as sculling champion of the Tyne.

Then it was Harry's turn. He said he was speaking on behalf of himself and his crew and expressed the great gratification that he felt at being invited to dine with the club, many of whom he had so long known as supporters of aquatic sports. He told of the pride he felt at having 'beaten the field' for the Champion Four-Oared Race at the last Royal Thames National Regatta, and the pleasure it would give if he or his son could be of any service to the club in the future. He finished his speech by saying that with proper training he and his crew would go up against any crew that might challenge them. He resumed his seat amidst loud cheers. His son John Hawks, cox Richard Clasper and Winship, the other member of the crew, each expressed their thanks in a few appropriate remarks. The night finished with everyone in a very happy frame of mind and Harry the toast of Tyneside!

It was now 1860, and Harry was once again on the move — this time back across the river to Gateshead. He had had various licensed premises in Newcastle over the years, and now took up residence at the Boat Inn, Pipewellgate from where he could view his beloved River Tyne. Life was always very busy for Harry, and the majority of it was taken up with his building of boats. He felt at this time, though, that more could be done for the safety of travellers at sea, and so became very interested in the design of lifeboats. Meanwhile, some of Harry's friends were working hard to arrange a match between Harry and an up-and-coming Thames waterman, George Drewitt. The choice of venue was haggled over, and it was eventually decided by the toss of a coin. Harry won, and the Tyne was chosen.

There was a great deal of difference in age between George Drewitt and Harry. Harry was forty-eight, George Drewitt was twenty-six. The race was to be rowed from the High Level to Scotswood Suspension Bridge, for a prize of £100 a side. A week prior to the race Drewitt arrived on Tyneside. He stayed with Mr Jewett, of Dunston, who had built his boat. Harry had built two boats for the race, one for calm water and the other in case it was rough.

The day of the race dawned fine with a wind favourable to a fast race. The crowds thronged the banks of both sides of the river, and the bridges were so packed that there was no space available for another body. To loud cheers from the crowd, Harry appeared from his boathouse and rowed directly into the middle of the river. A few minutes later Drewitt appeared. The race start was delayed because of the unruly behaviour of some of the steamboats carrying spectators. The *Express* steamed directly across the path the rowers were to take. But even her misconduct was exceeded by the *Newcastle* and other boats, as the race proceeded. The *Louise Crawshay*, being the boat selected for the conveyance of the umpires and referee, was of course entitled to a position where they could view the race. But in some parts the rowers could not be

Richard Clasper, Harry's brother, himself a first-class rower and a valued member of the championship crew.

The finish of a boat race at Scotswood Bridge. The race started from the High Level Bridge.

seen because of the boats which had got in front at the start. There was even more trouble when the steamboats *Catherine, Bon Accord* and *Amazon* steamed into the channel of the river before the start took place and preceded the official boat along the whole course. At one point a collision of these four boats took place, owing to their impeding the advance of the *Louise Crawshay*. Fortunately it was a slight accident but still serious enough to be a great deal of worry to the officials. The *Amazon's* paddle-box was broken and as she leaned over towards the *Louise Crawshay* a number of passengers seemed in imminent danger of slipping overboard. Several people leaped off the *Amazon* and on to the *Louise Crawshay*. One man slipped overboard, but he managed to catch hold of the edge of the boat and stopped himself falling into the river. There were twelve steamers in all, heavily laden with spectators anxiously trying to get as good a view as possible of the race. Some people were even to be seen clinging to the steamer's funnels!

Having won the toss Harry decided to take the north side of the river, although this was of no real advantage. Finally, at 5.51 p.m. the race started. Harry went straight into the lead, but it didn't take long for Drewitt to pull level and draw ahead. Harry made a strong effort to pull ahead and slightly improved his position as he passed the Shot Tower. This did not last long, and Drewitt continued to pull further and further ahead. He eventually won by about three lengths. Harry's backers had no cause to complain about his performance, he was beaten by the youth and strength of his opponent.

Drewitt rowed to the steamer *Louise Crawshay* and was loudly cheered by all the spectators. A few minutes after he left the boat, a collection was taken up for Harry, the total collected was £7.8s. Harry rowed himself back home, where his family and friends greeted him with much applause. While he took his defeat gracefully, he did begin to think that his sculling days were over, and that in future he might concentrate more on the pairs or four-oared races.

The Claspers and their friends left for London and the Royal Thames National Regatta, which was due to take place on Tuesday 20 July and Wednesday 21 July. After a tedious passage they arrived at 9 p.m. on Monday, and took up residence at the Feathers Tavern, Wandsworth. Their preparation for this important regatta had been hindered by the illness of Bob Chambers, although he was expected to take his place in the boat. Edward Winship was also not in the best of health, after suffering from boils. The London crews had been in hard training to win back the title and Championship of the World. Harry's crew were known as the Lord Kilmorey Crew, and consisted of J. H. Clasper, E. Winship, R. Chambers and Harry himself as stroke. They battled their way through to the finals where they came up against the Thomas Crew (Putney) and the A. P. Lonsdale Crew (Manchester and Tyne).

The final turned out to be a farce, with the Lord Kilmorey Crew claiming they were fouled and so put out of the race, leaving the London crew easy winners. As Harry left very annoyed, the committee made what they thought to be a noble gesture and awarded them £10. This just added fuel to the fire of Harry's displeasure and he offered to row against both crews there and then for no stake at all. But both crews declined. It seemed there were some

The Kilmorey Crew in 1861. They are George Hammerton, John Tagg,
Edward Winship, Robert Chambers and Robert Clasper.

people prepared to go to all lengths to stop the Claspers winning. For when Harry and his son went to put their boat in the water for the pair-oared race, they found two small holes bored in the fore-end under the cover so as to stop them competing. It seemed Harry would have to think long and hard before taking another crew to London as he doubted if they would receive a fair deal.

A group of Harry's friends decided that they would get together and organize a testimonial, so that they could honour the man who had done so much for the art of skiff rowing. They organized weekly meetings to discuss various methods of collecting money and formed a committee to oversee all arrangements. The committee was made up of Harry's friends and some local influential people. A close friend of Harry's, Mr Thomas Pringle, was to act as chairman. The chairman expressed a hope that subscriptions would be received from all parts of the United Kingdom, and even as far away as Australia, where Harry also had many friends. It was hoped that with all their means of raising money they would have enough to buy a piece of property for Harry and his family. It was decided that the fund raising would run for about twelve months, and that the presentation would take place in June 1862. Mr J. Cooke of Whickham addressed the committee and suggested that they purchase:

> ... a piece of land as near as possible to the River Tyne, to build a house on, suitable for either a public or private dwelling, they would place a large marble slab over the entrance doorway, to contain a proper inscription, eulogizing the merits of the man; and at the same time have a niche or bracket, bearing a full size figure of Harry in his regatta costume, with emblems. In this way the public would not only present him with a useful and permanent testimonial, but also a memorial to commemorate the superiority of the Tyne. The workshops were to be of timber, but not too close to the dwelling house, in case of fire, yet near enough to be safe. This testimonial and memorial in order to be a permanent heirloom to the family and public, had to be secured from being sold, mortgaged, given away, let, or otherwise disposed of; the proprietor was bound to keep it secure.

It seemed to be a great idea and everyone was fully behind the plan to raise enough money to buy Harry a large property of his own. It was agreed, and collections were started immediately. The money started to flood in from all areas, it seemed that everyone wanted to make some donation to their hero. Meanwhile Harry himself was a very busy man. He accompanied John Hawks to London for his race against young Pocock, which was to take place on the Thames on 9 July. The race was never in doubt from the start and John, like his father in the past, carried off the laurels with an easy win. Harry was still competing in races on rivers up and down the country as well as continuing to build the beautiful craft for which he was renowned.

The organized testimonial for Harry was now picking up speed, reflecting on the hard work being done by his friends. The large number of subscriptions received proved how highly Harry was thought of by all classes of society.

A plaster statue of Harry Clasper in his rowing kit. The statue was made in 1859 by Richard Haddrick and stands 3 feet tall.

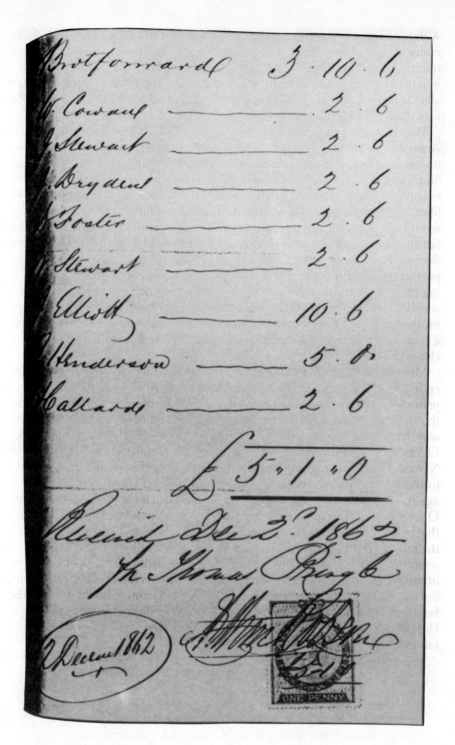

Brot forward	3 . 10 . 6
W. Coward	2 . 6
J. Stewart	2 . 6
J. Dryden	2 . 6
J. Foster	2 . 6
W. Stewart	2 . 6
J. Elliott	10 . 6
Henderson	5 . 0
Callard	2 . 6
	£ 5 . 1 . 0

Received Dec 3d 1862
Jh. Thomas Pringle

2 Decem 1862

List of money donated for Harry Clasper's testimonial in 1862.

48

Although some of the subscriptions were small, it has to be remembered that many were from working class people whose circumstances did not allow them to contribute larger sums. Yet the list showed in full measure the esteem in which he was held by men of his own class. Many knew and remembered all that he had done for the sport of skiff racing and for his beloved Tyne. He was their proud representative.

The committee gathered weekly at the home of Mr J. Bagnall of the Scotch Arms Inn in the Bigg Market, to discuss the progress of the testimonial. At one such meeting it was announced by the secretary, Mr Pringle, that Mr Stanley of the Tyne Concert Hall would arrange a concert for the following evening with all proceeds going towards the testimonial. The whole of Mr Stanley's company would appear during the evening and on the occasion would sing several pieces appropriate to the evening's entertainment. Mr Smith, of the Victoria Concert Rooms, and Mr Donald, of the Grainger Concert Rooms, had kindly agreed to allow their troupes to be incorporated in the performance. Although there were to be quite a few concerts of this type taking place, with the money raised going to the testimonial fund, the big event was booked for 5 June, at Mr Bamburgh's Wheat Sheaf Music Hall. The committee had by this time found a suitable piece of land, and were hoping within a few weeks to have all the transactions completed and the property purchased.

Meanwhile Harry was taking part in a novel race, which unfortunately ended in disagreement. The boats concerned were two model yachts, each restricted to 13 inches in the keel. A suitable piece of water was found to sail the small craft and soon the race took place. It had to be said that both craft were beautifully made by their respective owners — Harry Clasper and James Elliot. The intention of the race was to sail both craft across the river from Newcastle to the Haughs near Dunston. Soon after the start Harry's craft ran to the windward but she was stopped and turned into her proper course again, and ultimately touched the opposite shore a few seconds before Mr Elliot's model. The latter, however, objected to the winner on the grounds that by turning his boat Harry should have lost the match, and in consequence the race should be sailed over again. This time Mr Elliot's yacht was the first over, but Harry was so convinced of the superiority of his own model he offered to sail against Elliot's yacht a further mile giving him 100 yards start, but this was declined. It was obvious Elliot did not want to risk his new-found fame but he did agree to another race, this time against a model belonging to Harry's son, John Hawks. After a close-fought race John was the victor and James Elliot knew it was not to be his day.

5
HARRY'S TESTIMONIAL

It was the evening of 5 June and the night of Harry's testimonial. A special song had been written for the event and was published in the *Newcastle Daily Chronicle*:

> Times tries aw, they say, and they're not see far rang
> Noo he's myed a tyuff trial, he's tested lang —
> Aw meen Harry Clasper that weel chorised nyem,
> For aw'se sure they'res nee body can coupled wi' shyem.
> Faithful awd Harry — plucky as iver
> The still bloomen posey iv wor coaly river.
>
> Time's tried aw his dodges and says he's aw square.
> Byeth iv' mind and iv' body — he's soond ivry where;
> Nee better man iver tyuck hawd iv an oar.
> Nor can he fynd fault wiv'im when he's ashore.
>   Faltless awd Harry, &c.
>
> Tyeck him aw in aw, as wise Shakespeare says,
> (A've clean forgot where — but its yen iv his plays)
> Ye'll not fynd his equal in tyems or in Tyne,
> For in life or in deeth Harry Clasper ill shine.
>   Matchless awd Harry, &c.
>
> While larrels are still hangen thick roon'd his brow,
> He's tyun iv his heed for to bid ye adieu,
> He thinks i' the young 'uns that're fond i' the scull,
> And te ge' them a chance he's ne mair gen to pull,
>   Thoughtful awd Harry, &c.
>
> For the honours he brought; to wor canny awd Tyne,
> Folks talk about givin' him somethen that's fine,
> A smart testimonial — an' aw think it's but fiar,
> For whe can ye find that deserves a yen mair.
>   Then canny awd Harry, &c.

Noo leuk what he's dyun i' the boat rowen way,
What fine skiffs he myed — ay the best i' the day,
An' leuk what a man he's train'd intiv his place,
De ye think there's a chep dur row Chambers a race?
   Wonderful Harry, &c.

Lets all try wor best an see if we can,
Raise somethen to say that we think him a man,
That's cheap iv respect, if to this ye agree,
To show yet are willin' join in chorus wi me.
   Spirited Harry, &c.

If we div't behave weel tiv him, ye see,
His ghost, when he's deed, ill be seen fra the kee,
In a skiff, 'side the bridge, 'bout twelve iv'ry neet,
Till the mornin' cock craws, then he'll row oot iv' seet.
Worthy awd Harry, the pride o'wor river,
Yer nyem will flourish when y've gyen for iver.

It seemed as though it was going to be a great night; the hall was packed with many of Harry's friends from both his working and his rowing life. A beautiful skiff, built by Harry himself, was suspended horizontally over the select boxes, and on the stage were models of the first *St Agnes* (the original boat he used to take on the London watermen), *The Five Brothers*, and other craft of various ages. These were surrounded by flags and trophies. Around the walls were plates commemorating many of the celebrated skiff rowers of the Tyne, including the Claspers and Chambers. It was obvious that Mr Bamburgh and the committee had spared nothing to make the night a great success.

The performances were varied, including comedy acts, singing and orchestral music. A small boy danced remarkably well for a long time with full musical backing. Mr G. Hoskins sung 'Billy Patterson' and recited the curious adventures of Mr William Waters, of whose origin so little was known as to render it dubious whether or not he ever had any paternity! Messrs Lamb & Kitchen performed a comedy interlude and they were followed on stage by Mr Geordie Ridley, a noted singer of Tyneside songs. Mr Ridley sang the now famous song, 'Blaydon Races' — the first time this had been sung in public. A second song containing witty local allusions was also sung by Geordie Ridley, the principal portion of the ditty referring to the late contest between Harry and Drewitt. This song was loudly applauded. A newspaper account in the *Newcastle Daily Chronicle* reported the following:

Other songs in a similar vein were sung by other vocalists until 10 o'clock, when the principal part of the proceedings took place. With the band playing the tune of the 'Keel Row', the curtain rose and standing there were J. H. Clasper, R. Chambers, R. Clasper jun., Winship and Harry Clasper, all in boating costume, and each holding an oar upright in his hand. The audience went wild, and the clapping was hard and long. The costumes looked smart and neat and the men presented an appearance of so much strength and manly vigour as to convince any spectator that the supremacy of the Tyne was perfectly safe under their care. The men were accompanied by Mr Pringle and Mr J. Bagnall, both of whom had taken an active part in the promotion of the testimonial.

Mr Pringle made a short speech, thanking all those who had come there that evening to honour Harry Clasper. He carried on saying 'the North Country was exceedingly proud of her oarsmen, and she never could have held the proud and prominent position of the championship which she held now, if it had not been for the strength and perseverance of Harry.' Again loud cheers went around the room. Having alluded to the old skiffs now built after Harry's models, Mr Pringle described the defeat of the Londoners by the Claspers, and went on to say that since then the championship might be said never to have left the Tyne. Though London had a population of two million people, it could not boast of the bone and muscles of Tyneside, as presented by Chambers, Harry and the Claspers. Once again the cheers were deafening as Mr Pringle thanked the audience as the curtain fell.

This did not signal the end of Harry's career, for both training and boat building were to take up more of his time, and he still felt fit and strong enough to compete and win many more races. His stamina was put to the test when along with his son, John, E. Winship, R. Chambers and R. Clasper, he went down to take part in a race at Putney. After reaching the finals they came up against two London crews and a hard struggle ensued. Once again the honours were brought back to Tyneside.

The following week the testimonial committee met at Mr Bagnall's Scotch Arms Inn. It was good news. They had at last purchased the property which they could make into a hotel and present to Harry. The property was situated at No. 1 Armstrong Street, Scotswood Road, and contained ten rooms. Although it only had a beer licence, the committee still had to pay £605 to secure the place. The drawback was the need for a spirit licence as well, but this too was easily overcome thanks to the local magistrates. The idea of the committee was to ensure that he had somewhere for his family and himself to live when he did eventually retire. The committee felt it should in some way bear the name of Clasper, and it was eventually decided that the 'Clasper Hotel' was most appropriate.

The Claspers were now taking a long-earned rest from rowing, although this was mainly forced upon them owing to John Hawks being very poorly. The lads had had a hectic season and now they could concentrate on building new boats and making fresh challenges. Harry was also spending a lot of time training his young son-in-law George Strong, who was also a fine oarsman.

Thursday, 27 November 1862 was the day chosen for the official handing over of Harry's new property. A group of about forty of his friends gathered at his new home, the Clasper Hotel. It was hard to believe that it was only a year or so ago that the idea to commemorate the great oarsman and boat builder had first been thought of. Following the various toasts made to the

The Clasper Arms was once named the Clasper Hotel. This was the building presented to Harry at his testimonial in 1862.

53

Harry Clasper in the 1860s.

Queen and the Prince of Wales, etc., the chairman stood up and gave his speech. In this he congratulated Harry on his many years at the aquatic sport, and his great victories, especially against the men from the Thames. He concluded by giving a toast to Harry, which was followed by loud cheers by all who had attended the function. Harry in responding to this speech assured those present that his whole aim had been to 'improve the principles of boat building and rowing'. He concluded by thanking his friends for the services they had rendered to him in arranging his testimonial. The health of the secretary, Mr Pringle, was next proposed by the vice-chairman. The evening was going with a swing.

It was then the turn of Mr Pringle to stand and make a speech. After praising the committee and public for all their hard work in raising the subscriptions for their hero Harry he went on to ask them to continue in their efforts as there was still quite a sum of money needed to complete all transactions. Mr Pringle continued his speech, commenting on how he felt that the Tyne watermen were still far superior to any others. In fact, he was sure that 'Englishmen as a whole were better than the rest of the world in aquatic sports'.

Other members of the committee proposed various toasts, including the 'Champion Four of England', and Robert Chambers — 'Champion Sculler of England'. After the storm of applause and cheering had subsided Chambers rose and thanked his numerous friends for the honour they had conferred on him and assured the company that instead of the 'absurd trash that had appeared in one of the London sporting papers that he was afraid to meet a Londoner, he was willing to meet any number, aye, a dozen if they would give him fair play'. But he remarked that the die was cast, and that in future the Cockneys would have to work on equal footings with the provincials, and unless they allowed expenses they mght have to keep the empty title. Chambers sat down amidst loud cheers, and the toasts carried on. They finally ended with a toast to the health of John Hawks Clasper, Harry's eldest son, followed by three rousing cheers. The company then dispersed making their way very happily home no doubt!

The following is an abstract of the accounts:

	£	s.	d.
Subscriptions Received	159	10	3
Subscriptions not Received	73	1	0
Subscriptions in All	244	10	6
Money already Expended	190	3	9
Cost of House	605	0	0
Now Worth	1000	0	0

Mortgage to Building Society Nine Years to Run.

6
DEATH OF THE CHAMPION

The challenges still kept coming in to Harry and his crew. One came from the pitmen of Blyth in December 1862. The race to be rowed in 'cobles' for £50 or £100 a side. The terms were agreed by both sides, but had to be cancelled the following week on account of the colliery at which the pitmen worked being put on short time. But it was hoped that as soon as circumstances changed, the match would be on again.

Harry was now in his fiftieth year and although still in tremendous shape, was racing less and less. He carefully chose his races and they were mainly against local men. Most of his time was spent coaching his very close friend Robert Chambers, and son-in-law George Strong, although he was often seen on the river in the company of his son John Hawks. John was in fact fast becoming a very fine oarsman, and through watching and helping his father in the boat house had picked up the fine art of boat building himself. In 1864 John moved to Durham and took up residence at Paradise House, an establishment by the side of the River Wear, to carry on his work.

Things went along as usual for the Clasper family until 4 June 1868, when the sad news hit Tyneside, and Harry in particular, that his very close friend and able pupil Robert Chambers had died at his home in St Anthony's, Walker. Bob was only 37 years of age and was probably the greatest natural sculler the world had ever seen. He was the first Tyne oarsman that had ever won the proud title of the Champion of the World. Bob had not been the strongest of men, although to see him rowing no one would have thought it. He died of tuberculosis, a common disease among the industrial working class in the North East. It seems this could have been a legacy from his time with the Hawks' Tyneside Iron Foundry. Bob's funeral was a very sad affair. The Tyne had lost a champion and a friend and it was estimated that between 50 000 and 60 000 people were assembled along the funeral route. Harry was unable to attend the funeral as he himself was ill and confined to bed.

But life had to go on, and the Tyne men had to pick themselves up and look

Paradise House in Durham. This was the home of John Hawks Clasper from 1864.

DURHAM.

JOHN H. CLASPER,

BOAT BUILDER,

Begs to inform Rowing Clubs and the Aquatic public generally, that after ten years' practical experience with his Father, H. CLASPER, the inventor of the present Outrigger, he has commenced business on his own account at Durham; and having secured very commodious premises, he has every facility for building, on the shortest notice, Racing or Pleasure Boats of the most approved model, for combining speed with durability.

TERMS FORWARDED ON APPLICATION.

J. H. C. IS OPEN TO TRAIN GENTLEMEN FOR PRIVATE OR OTHER MATCHES.

N. B.—Boats let out on hire, and a stock of New and Second-hand Boats constantly on hand for Sale.

Advertisement from The Almanack of 1863 for John Hawks Clasper's boat building business.

for a new champion. There were some fine young rowers, but to replace Chambers would not be easy. One young man however, named James Renforth, was starting to make a name for himself.

However, sadness seemed to follow sadness for the great Tyne rowers and the Clasper family in particular. They were just recovering from the sad loss of Bob Chambers, when they were once again plunged into deep sorrow. It was Saturday 24 April 1869, when William Clasper, who was the ferryman at Benwell Boat House, finished work at 9.30 p.m. and went in his boat to Swalwell for a drink with his friends. This is where he stayed until about 11.30 p.m., when he left to return home. When he didn't arrive home his wife and friends became very concerned. It wasn't until the following morning that the news came through. His body was found alongside his boat at Derwenthaugh Gut. It seems that he had not been rowing his boat but 'powying' or punting himself down with a boat hook which had probably slipped causing him to fall into the water. No one witnessed the accident for he had been on his own when this had happened. His body was found lying by the waterside when the tide went down. He was taken immediately to a neighbouring public house where he lay to await the coroner's inquest. William, although the eldest of the brothers and at that time sixty years old, was still very fit and strong.

The coroner's inquest followed on Monday 26 April and was held at Mrs Jane Walker's Skiff Inn at Derwenthaugh. After hearing the evidence of Christopher Bainbridge, who had been with William earlier on the Saturday night and had set him to his boat, and also the evidence of John Oxley, a coke burner who found the body on Sunday morning, the jury returned a verdict of 'Found Drowned'. The funeral followed on Tuesday 27 April and Harry led the mourners to the place of burial at St Mary's churchyard, Whickham. This was the second brother Harry had lost to his beloved Tyne.

Harry had by this time left the Clasper Hotel, after many happy years living there. The place had become too big for him and Susannah since the majority of their family had married and left home, and running costs were very high. After a short stay at the Barley Mow Inn in the Milk Market he took up residence at the Tunnel Inn, Tyne Street on the east side of the city. He ran the inn with the help of his wife. It was a very busy place, situated close to the entrance to the Victoria Tunnel, hence its name. The tunnel was built to convey coal in moving tubs from the Spital Tongues Colliery to ships moored by the river's edge. Harry enjoyed working in his bar where he could converse with his friends about the past and present rowing matches. Because his residence was very close to the river, it was always full of customers who had close connections with the water, and this kept him very much in touch with river life. And although his champion crew would never be forgotten, Harry knew the reputation of the river would be in safe hands with James Renforth and his crew: Winship, Taylor and John Martin.

It was at his residence in Tyne Street that on Thursday 8 July 1870, Harry was seized by a mysterious illness, and had to retire to his bed. It seemed there was nothing in his indisposition to create too much alarm. He had been to Durham to watch the regatta, and the previous week he had been with some friends

John Hawks Clasper in 1864.

James Renforth.

enjoying the Carlisle Races. And only a few evenings prior to this he had been at the most popular concert room in town, Bamburgh's. However, by Sunday he seemed much worse, and appeared to be having convulsions. His wife Susannah immediately sent for the assistance of his general practitioner, Dr May. When he arrived he found Harry to be in a low, nervous state but not bad enough to cause his family and friends any great concern. Throughout Monday Harry became much worse and by Tuesday he was gradually sinking. At 10 a.m. he passed quietly and peacefully to rest in the presence of his wife, family and a few close friends. His doctor pronounced that death was from 'congestion of the brain'.

The news of Harry's death quickly spread across the town. Grown men were seen to be in tears when they heard the sad news. Their Harry, their champion, who took on and often beat all challengers, was gone. His son John arrived from London the following day to help make the funeral arrangements, and after a consultation with his mother and other members of the family, they agreed to comply with the request of some of his father's old friends that the funeral should take place on the following Sunday. The interment was to be at St Mary's Church, Whickham. This would give Harry's numerous friends the opportunity to pay their last respects to his memory. Edward Winship, who was a close friend of Harry's, and himself a great rower, was at the time in London watching a match between Kelly, Champion of the Thames, and Sadler. When told of the news he was deeply shocked. He telegraphed John to say that he would leave for Newcastle at once, so that he could be present at the funeral. The arrangements first proposed for the funeral were altered two days before, after a meeting of some of Harry's friends. It was at first arranged that the funeral procession would go by road, from Harry's home in Ouseburn to the churchyard in Whickham. Then it was decided that part of the journey to his last resting place would be over the waters of the river he loved dearly, and for which he had worked so persistently and successfully. The procession would not go along the Quayside as was at first suggested, as the partially unfinished work of the Riverside Railway would interfere with the progress of the mourning coaches. All the planning was eventually completed. It was hoped that members of the public would turn out to pay their last respects to a great man.

The day of the funeral arrived but never for a moment did anyone anticipate such a display as was witnessed. Invitations had been extended to watermen and other supporters of aquatics, but it was the number of townspeople who turned out en masse to show their respect for their hero that showed he was idolized by the local people. Although the funeral procession was to set off at 2.45 p.m. people started to assemble at least two hours earlier than this, in the neighbourhood of the Tunnel Inn. They were clambering for every possible vantage point to watch the cortège leave and the little cobbled street became packed. Fortunately for all parties involved the day was beautiful, fine and bright though the sun at times was almost too hot. As well as the heat the passing breeze created clouds of dust to add to the discomfort, but still people continued to pour into Tyne Street. Eventually the narrow street became so crowded that everything came to a standstill. The topic of most conversations seemed to be of the many

The Barley Mow, where Harry once lived. This pub is still in use today.

Tyne Street, where Harry Clasper lived, and where he died in 1870. His funeral procession came up this street and on to the new road.

great victories their 'Harry' had fought and won for the honour of Tyneside. There could be no doubt that many of the rising oarsmen who thronged the veteran's doorway would in future try to emulate his many qualities.

Henry Kelly, a champion sculler of the Thames, was unfortunately unable to attend the funeral, but those who knew Kelly realized it had to be something important to keep him away from Tyneside at this time. Kelly had a great deal of respect for all Northern rowers, but especially Harry. Amongst the mourners assembled on the open space in front of the old-fashioned inn were many of the most famous oarsmen of the day. Edward Winship, one of Harry's racing partners, and Renforth's champion four-oared crew were all there. His backers also patiently waited side by side with some of the friends Harry had made over the years for the moment when the rapidly forming processon was ready to move off on its journey.

A little before 3 p.m. the coffin was carried to the door and conveyed on the shoulders of six of Harry's very close rowing friends to the beautiful hearse which had been furnished by Mr Slater of St Thomas Street, Newcastle. There was no singing or prayers as the body was brought forward, but when the public saw the black-coated coffin covered with fresh flowers, many eyes were filled with tears on this sad and solemn occasion.

The pall bearers, Mr James Renforth, Mr James Taylor, Mr Thomas Winship, Mr John Martin, Mr Thomas Taylor and Mr Edward Winship, then took up their positions on either side of the hearse, which was pulled by four caparisoned (black plumed) horses. Everything was ready. Mr Stephenson's excellent band moved to the front of the hearse and started to play the grand and impressive music of the 'Dead March' from *Saul* under the leadership of Mr Ure. The cortège then moved slowly up Tyne Street. Behind the hearse followed about two hundred local oarsmen and members of the Tyne Rowing Clubs. Following these were four morning coaches containing Harry's relatives and close friends, then more friends walking three abreast behind this. These were followed by twenty private carriages and other vehicles wth the general public bringing up the rear on foot. The local police had great difficulty in keeping the thoroughfare clear to allow the procession to make headway.

The route was from Tyne Street via New Road (now City Road), Gibson Street, New Bridge Street, Grey Street and Dean Street to the river's edge, where the cortège was taken on board tug boats to Derwenthaugh. From there the path was to lead over the cinder heaps to Swalwell and then uphill to the west end of Whickham, a distance of 7 or 8 miles. Although the route covered a long distance it was lined with people all the way along, everyone wanting to pay their last respects to a very great man. It was truly a grand and impressive sight to witness and one which Harry would never have dreamt of during his lifetime. It was remembered by some that Harry was ill in bed when his close friend and champion rower Robert Chambers died and was carried to his grave. After being told of the scenes that were witnessed then, Harry expressed an opinion that his own career would be forgotten when he died, and that his funeral would be much more simple and quiet than that of his successful pupil. But this was to be proved incorrect. Every window and doorway along the route

Harry Clasper's funeral procession.

was filled. Every flag that could be seen on the vessels in the river was at half mast and expressions of sympathy and regret were freely uttered by everyone. Along New Bridge Street were scenes of a similar character. The vast space in front of the almshouse, the surroundings of St Agnes' Church, the steps of the Jubilee schools and the walls bordering the roadway were filled with people, while the wide thoroughfare itself was crowded with no room to move. Turning into Gibson Street the sight was even busier. Every window was open and spectators could be seen two or three deep inside each house. Some daring youngsters had even managed to climb to the top of lamp posts for the the best view possible. Every available inch of space whether on doorsteps, footpaths or the pavement was used. All along New Bridge Street the scene was the same, there was not a window or garden that wasn't crowded with occupants. Going down past Adelaide Place to the bridge an excellent view could be obtained of the route as far as Trinity Presbyterian Chapel, and there was concern for the number of people crammed into it.

Slowly and solemnly the vast procession moved towards Sandhill with the bells from St Nicholas' and St Andrew's mingling with the strains from the band. The hearse at last reached the Sandhill after its long, difficult journey, but still had to be moved through large crowds of people which proved an almost impossible task. A strong detachment of police were brought to the front of the procession and an opening was made along the Close to the Corporation Quay, where Harry's body was removed from the hearse for conveyance over the part of the old Tyne course that Harry had formerly rowed so frequently to victory. The proceedings were closely watched by thousands of people who had assembled on the High Level and Old Tyne Bridges, both of which became very congested. Many more people had congregated on the hillside beneath the tower of St Mary's Church in Gateshead, and on the quays and wharves bordering both sides of the river.

The coffin was carried on board the steam tug *Robert Chambers*, followed by relatives and close friends. The vessel then quickly moved off into mid-channel to await the boarding of many other friends on to the steam tugs *Louise Crawshay*, *Mary Jane*, *Joseph Cowan*, *Margaret* and *Prince of Wales*. Many people agreed that it was a fitting way to carry a waterman to his grave. They were pleased to think that the vessel which carried Harry to his final resting place should bear the name of his closest friend.

As the tugs passed the end of the Mansion House a hymn wafted across the water from a party of choristers who had stationed themselves on some timber at the river's edge. Another large crowd had assembled at Skinner Burn to watch the procession go by and a continuous stream of people ran along the quays and haughs in line with the steam tugs on the north side and along the Rabbit Banks and fields on the south. Groups of people congregated at all points on the shore and young oarsmen sculled their boats rapidly along the water all forming a strangely impressive sight never before witnessed.

After a short time the boats ran up to the quays at Derwenthaugh where Harry had spent many years of his life as a coke burner. His body was then taken on shore and carried over the dusty heaps behind the ovens to the hearse which was waiting on the road. The Durham Police, under the leadership of Superintendent Squires, had done a grand job to keep the road clear and it was now their job to see Harry reach his final resting place. The procession was joined by the keelmen of the Stella Coal Company, Messrs Cowen & Company's Works, Mr Ramsay's Works and others generally employed at Stella, Blaydon and Derwenthaugh. They accompanied the procession for the remainder of the journey. The route lay across the Derwent to Swalwell then on to Whickham. Here too the villagers turned out in great numbers as Harry had been well respected by these people.

They reached the gates of Whickham church precisely three hours after their departure from Tyne Street. The churchyard and the church tower itself were crowded and every available spot that would give a view of the proceedings was occupied. The coffin was taken off the hearse and carried into the churchyard. The following words were said by the clergyman as Harry's body was brought within the bounds of the consecrated ground: 'I am the resurrection and the life'. The crowds who thronged the churchyard at the same time pressed forward into the sacred area so that there was no room to move. They all preserved the deepest silence as the funeral party entered the church; and the Rev. Mr Taylor, on reading the lesson, impressed upon the large number of mourners the solemnity of the service in which they were taking part.

The last resting place of the veteran was soon reached. Henry Clasper was laid to rest near to the grave of his parents and two of his brothers, Edward and John. Harry's relatives gathered around the grave while the Rev. B. Carr read the closing passages of the burial service. There were few but the immediate relatives and friends at the graveside got a glimpse of the coffin for as soon as they departed the grave was closed. It was a truly sad day and many tears were shed over the grave of the departed oarsman. All who were present in the pretty secluded churchyard must have been impressed with the appropriateness of the spot of Harry's final resting place. For just down the steep slope from the graveyard lay the village of Dunston where Harry was born. Further on, the River Tyne could be seen. This was where many a hard-fought race and well-won victory had taken place. The river upon which he had earned his reputation and was feared by those who couldn't match his courage, skill and prowess with the oars.

It was a long time before the churchyard resumed its tranquillity, as people wandered home tearful and dejected. The whole day had been a magnificent tribute to an ordinary man who had done his best for his profession and his beloved Tyneside. It was estimated that between 100 000 and 130 000 people had witnessed the proceedings.

Harry's friends raised enough money to build a grand monument over his grave which still stands today, and bears the following inscription:

Beneath this monument raised to his memory, by
ardent affection of friends and admirers from every
class and from all parts of the Kingdom, and in this
sacred spot commanding a full view of that noble river,

the well beloved scene of former triumphs rest
the mortal remains of Henry (Harry) Clasper, the
accomplished oarsman, and boat builder of
Derwenthaugh, who died July 12th, 1870, aged 58 years.
Know ye not that they which run in a race run all,
but one receiveth the prize.
So run that ye may obtain. 1 Cor. IX,24.

The memorial to Harry Clasper in Whickham Cemetery.

APPENDIX – RACE SUMMARY, 1841–1860

These are just some of Harry's and his crews' great races from 1841 to 1860.

1841 June   — Won scullers' race, Durham Regatta; prize withheld

1842 July 16 — With three brothers; beaten by Coombes' crew, fours, £300, Newcastle

1843 Aug. 7 — With three brothers; won purse £525, fours, Tyne Regatta
            7 — Won scullers' race; Silver Cup, Tyne Regatta
     Sept. 2 — Beaten by John Bell's crew, fours, £20, Newcastle
     Oct.   7 — With three brothers; beat S. Danson's crew, fours, £50, Newcastle
          14 — With three brothers; beat John Bell's crew, fours, £80, Newcastle

1844 June 21 — With two brothers and Hawks; won £50, Thames Regatta
     June 22 — With two brothers and Hawks; beaten by Coombes' crew, fours, £100, Thames Regatta. Outriggers first introduced on the Thames by Clasper
     Aug. 15 — With three brothers; won fours, £30, Newcastle and Gateshead Regatta
          16 — Won scullers' prize; Newcastle and Gateshead Regatta
     Dec. 18 — Beaten by R. Coombes; sculls, £180, Newcastle

1845 June 26 — With two brothers and Hawks; won fours, £100, Thames Regatta
     July 21 — With two brothers; won fours, North of England Regatta
         21 — Won scullers' prize; North of England Regatta
     Sept. 29 — Beat Carrol; sculls, £200, Mersey, easy
     Nov. 19 — Presented with Testimonial
     Nov. 25 — Beat W. Pocock; sculls, £200, Newcastle

1846 June 22 — Beaten by Newell; sculls, £200, Newcastle
     July 27 — With two brothers and Hawks; won two fours, prize £25 each, Manchester Regatta
     Sept. 3 — With three brothers; won fours, £50, North of England Regatta
          4 — Beaten by Maddison; scullers' race, North of England Regatta

70

With brother William; won pairs, £10, North of
England Regatta

Nov. 16 — Rowed Maddison; sculls, £200, Newcastle. Dispute

1847 June 21 — With J. Clasper; won pairs, Durham Regatta
Aug. 11 — With R. Clasper; beaten by R. and T. Coombes, pairs,
£200, Putney to Mortlake
Nov. 2 — Beaten by Maddison; sculls, £200, Newcastle

1848 June 26 — With R. Clasper; won pairs, Durham Regatta
26 — With two brothers and Wilkinson; won fours, Durham
Regatta
July 20 — With two brothers; won fours, £100, Thames Regatta

1849 June — With three brothers; won fours, Durham Regatta
With R. Clasper; won pairs, Durham Regatta
July — With R. Clasper and T. Coombes; won fours, £100,
Thames Regatta
Aug. — With three brothers; won fours, Stockton Regatta

1850 June — With three brothers; won fours, Talkin Tarn
With three brothers; won fours, Talkin Tarn
Beaten by Candlish; sculls, £10, Talkin Tarn
With R. Clasper; won pairs, Talkin Tarn
With R. Clasper; won pairs, Members' Plate, Durham
With three brothers; won fours, Patrons' Plate, Durham
Aug. — With two brothers and Salter; won two fours,
£20, Manchester Regatta
With two brothers and Salter; won two fours, £25, Ellesmere
Plate
Sept. — With three brothers; won two fours, Patrons' Plate, Tees
Regatta
With W. Clasper; won pairs, Tees Regatta
With three brothers; won Tradesmen's Plate, fours, Tees
Regatta
Beat Candlish; sculls, Tees Regatta
Oct. 21 — Beaten by Candlish; Belt and Purse, £20, Tyne
Beat Anthony Maddison; Tyne Champion Belt, £20, Tyne

1851 June — Beaten; fours, Henley, £100, broke thowl
With three brothers; beat R. Coombes, fours, £40, Henley
With five brothers, J. Messenger, W. Pocock and T. Coles;
beat Bower's and Taylor's crews
With three brothers; won Patrons' Plate, fours, Durham
Aug. — With two brothers and Hawks; won fours, £20, Talkin Tarn
With R. Clasper; beaten by J. and W. Taylor, pair oared,
Talkin Tarn
Won scullers' prize, Talkin Tarn

Sept. 9 — Beaten by Candlish; sculls, £200 and Champion of the Tyne, foul

1852 Aug.   — Beaten by M. Taylor; skiffs, Nottingham
Beaten by Taylors, pairs, Nottingham

10 — With three brothers; beaten by Taylor's crew, fours, £100, Manchester Regatta
R. Clasper beat Carrol in final heat
With R. Clasper; beaten by Wood and Ault, pairs, £10, Manchester Regatta
With W. Clasper; beaten by J. and G. Taylor, pairs, £10, Talkin Tarn
With three brothers; won fours, £20, Talkin Tarn
With W. Clasper; beaten by M. and T. Taylor, pairs, Talkin Tarn
Beaten by Candlish, by mistaking the buoy, sculls, £8, Talkin Tarn

Sept.   — With Wood; won beating the Taylors, pairs, £40, Chester Regatta

1853 Jan.   1 — With three brothers; beaten by Elswick crew, fours, £100, Newcastle

May 24 — Beaten by Pocock, sculls, £100, Putney to Chiswick
Another match; Clasper received £25 forfeit

June   — With brothers; beaten by Taylors, fours, Durham Regatta
Won sculls (Wear stake); Durham Regatta
Beaten by Taylors, pairs, Durham Regatta
Beaten by Winship and Bruce, Durham Regatta

Aug.   — Beaten by Candlish, sculls, £10, Nottingham Regatta
With Ault, Wood and Davidson; won fours, £40, Nottingham Regatta
With Ault, Wood and Davidson; won fours, £50, Manchester Regatta
With Ault, Wood and Davidson; beaten, fours, £60, Chester Regatta
With Ault, Wood and Davidson; won two fours, Glasgow

1854 Feb.   9 — With Candlish; beat Winship and Bruce, pairs, £200, Tyne

June   — With two brothers and Wood; won fours, £20, Durham Regatta
Won scullers' prize, Durham Regatta

Aug.   — Won scullers' prize, Talkin Tarn
With Maddison; won pairs, Talkin Tarn
With T. Clasper, Wood and Maddison; won fours, Steward's Cup and £20, Talkin Tarn

Aug. 9 — Beat Robert Newell easily (receiving 2 lengths' start), sculls, £100, Putney to Mortlake
With Pocock; won pairs, Thames National Regatta

With T. Clasper, Wood and Maddison; beaten, fours, £100, Thames National Regatta
With T. Clasper, Wood and Maddison; won fours, prize £40, Thames National Regatta
With Winship, Davidson, Bruce, Maddison, Cook, T. Clasper and Wood; beat Cole, R. Coombes, Mackinney, T. Coombes, T. Mackinney, Newell, Goodrun, Kelly; eights, £27, London Regatta Course, North versus South, Thames National Regatta

1855 Aug.   — With mixed crew; beaten, fours, £100, Thames National Regatta
Beaten, scullers' race in final heat, Thames National Regatta
Beaten by Landsmen's fours, fouled and disqualifed
With Pocock; beaten by Bruce and Winship, pairs, Thames National Regatta
Won Championship Prize, sculls, £20, Tyne Regatta

1856 Feb. 14 — Presented with a Testimonial by his Newcastle friends
Mar. 24 — Beat T. Taylor, sculls, £80 a side, Tyne
June   — With R. and J. H. Clasper and Chambers; won fours, £20, Durham
With J. H. Clasper; won pairs, Durham
Aug.   — With Pocock; beaten by Winship and Bruce, pairs, Thames National Regatta
With Pocock, Chambers and Mackinney; won fours, £100, Thames National Regatta

1857 Aug.   — With J. H. Clasper, A. Maddison and Chambers; won fours, £100, Thames National Regatta
Beaten by Ault, Wood, Winship and Bruce; a close and gallant race, Manchester. Clasper broke an oar
Aug. 28 — With Chambers, Ault and Winship; won fours, Manchester Regatta. Week after beat Taylor's crew at Lancaster

1858 June   — With J. H. Clasper; won pairs, Durham Regatta
Claspers beat Taylors; fours, Durham Regatta
Claspers beat Taylors; fours, £100, Tyne
Claspers received £50 forfeit from J. Mackinney
July 22 — Beat R. Campbell; sculls, £200 and Championship of Scotland, Clyde
With Chambers, T. Mackinney and T. Pocock; fours, £100, Thames National Regatta
Oct.   6 — Beat R. Campbell; £200, Championship, Loch Lomond
Nov.   9 — Beaten by Thomas White; £200, Thames

1859 June 27 — With J. H. Clasper; beat Chambers and Winship, pairs, Durham Regatta

28 — With J. H. Clasper, Chambers and Winship; won fours, Durham Regatta

Aug. — With J. H. Clasper, Chambers and Winship; won fours, Champion Prize, £100, Thames National Regatta

23 — With J. H. Clasper, Chambers and Winship; won fours, Manchester Regatta

1860 June 18 — With J. H. Clasper, Chambers and Winship; fours, £23, prize shared with Taylor's crew, Durham Regatta

July 21 — With J. H. Clasper, Chambers and Winship; beaten, fours, £100, Thames Regatta. Fouled by Thames and Shakespeare crews

26 — With J. H. Clasper, Chambers and Winship; won fours, Derby Regatta

Aug. 27 — With J. H. Clasper, Chambers and Winship; won fours, Manchester Regatta

Sept. 27 — With J. H. Clasper, Chambers and Winship; won fours, Newcastle and Gateshead Regatta

Clasper as a rower never had an equal. By 1860 his number of contests bordered on 130. His winnings amounted to about £2586. Of this £1655 was won in four-oared races, £184 in pair-oared races and £747 in skiff races.

ACKNOWLEDGEMENTS

Firstly, I would like to thank Gateshead Libraries and Arts, in particular Patrick Conway and Alison Court, for their help and perseverance in bringing this book into print.

I would also like to thank the following, without whose help this book would not have been possible:

Newcastle Central Library, Local Studies; Tyne and Wear Archives, Blandford House; Northumberland Record Office, Melton Park; National Newspaper Library; Photographs by Malcolm Kirsopp and Tony Joyce; Sketches by Joan Murray; Sue Shaw. Also my many thanks to friends who have given their support in the writing of this book.

Finally, I would like to thank Newcastle-upon-Tyne City Libraries and Arts for the use of the map on pages 2–3, the Clasper v. Newell poster on page 25, the Thames regatta programme on page 40 and the testimonial money list on page 48. Thanks also to West Newcastle Local Studies for the photograph of the Clasper Arms on page 53.